SACRED MOUNTAINS
OF NORTHERN THAILAND
AND THEIR LEGENDS

DONALD K. SWEARER

SOMMAI PREMCHIT

PHAITHOON DOKBUAKAEW

Silkworm Books

Text © 2004 by Donald K. Swearer, Sommai Premchit and Phaithoon Dokbuakaew
Photographs © 1994–2002 by Donald K. Swearer, 1976 by Hans Penth

All rights reseved

No part of this publication may be reproduced, stored in a retrieval system, or transmitted, in any form or by any means, electronic, mechanical, photocopying, recording or otherwise, without the prior permission in writing of the publishing.

ISBN: 978-974-9575-48-2

First edition published in 2009 by
Silkworm Books
430/58 M. 7, T. Mae Hia, Chiang Mai 50100, Thailand
info@silkwormbooks.com
www.silkwormbooks.com

Typeset in Janson Text 10 pt. by Silk Type

Printed and bound in the United States by Lightning Source

In memory of Phra Phothirangsi
and
Khruemat Wuthikan
who fought to preserve Doi Suthep
as a sacred mountain

CONTENTS

PREFACE AND ACKNOWLEDGMENTS

Mountains are an omnipresent feature of northern Thailand's topography. They mark the boundaries of its fertile river valleys and are the source of its watersheds and formerly extensive teak forests. They provide the principal habitat for northern Thailand's diverse range of flora and fauna as well as hilltribe settlements, and the more recent incursion of luxury resorts and tourist destinations. But northern Thailand's mountains are much more than a topographic feature and a physical environment. These mountains are constitutive of northern Thai identity. The myths, legends, and history of the north connect primordial stories of the Buddha, guardian spirits, Brahmanical deities, and holy ascetics, with those who settled in northern Thailand and with its most important topographic feature—mountains. These peaks inspired fear and awe, respect and love, curiosity and creative imagination. They were—and to a lesser extent still are—constitutive of what it means to be a northern Thai, whether one lives in a town, a city, or a rural village. They define both the physical and mental landscape of the region.

Maps and guidebooks of northern Thailand reveal the degree to which mountains dominate the region. From a vast list, three might be mentioned for their current popularity with both Thai and foreign visitors. Doi Inthanon located in Chiang Mai's Chom Thong district, reaches to a height of 2,565 m (8,415 ft.) above sea level, and is the country's highest peak. Two *chedi*s honoring the king and queen of Thailand were constructed on their sixtieth birthdays near the summit in 1987 and 1992. The Phra That *chedi* located on Doi Tung, a 1,800-meter (5,900-foot) peak in Chiang Rai province, attracts thousands of pilgrims annually from Thailand, the Shan States in Myanmar, Laos, and elsewhere. Doi Ang Khang in Fang district has become a favorite tourist destination because of resorts built there following the opening of a Royal Project in 1969. Even more significant for their prominent place in the myths and legends of the region are Doi Suthep (1,601 m; 5,250 ft.) with which the city of Chiang Mai has been linked since the time of its founder, King Mangrai (1259–1317); Doi Kham, a modest peak in the Suthep-Pui range to the south of Doi Suthep off the road to Chom Thong; and Doi Chiang Dao (over 2,000 m; 7,000 ft.), known as Doi Ang Salung in the northern Thai chronicles (*tamnan*), situated north of Chiang Mai on the way to Fang. Because of their special place in the legendary history of the Chiang Mai region, I have selected these last three mountains as the focus of this study.

The translation of the narratives associated with Doi Ang Salung Chiang Dao, Doi Suthep, and Doi Kham included in this volume were undertaken not only because they represent the rich cultural heritage and narrative traditions of the region known as Lan Na (the land of a million rice paddies) or Yonok (the northern region), but because of the conviction that, if these stories fade from modern memory, the perduring meaning of northern Thailand itself will be lost. Rather than being a place filled with culturally constituted meaning and identity defining stories, the region will degenerate into a nameless, globalized space, a "virtual reality" of shopping malls, internet cafes, intrusive condominiums, and desecrated sacred spaces.

The first chapter explores the relationship between culture, particularly its religious dimensions, and the natural environment. It reflects the increasing commitment by religious practitioners and scholars of religion to reassess the ecological underpinnings of the world's religions, and in doing so to bring a humanistic perspective to the debates among scientists and policy makers regarding the nature of the global environmental crisis and its solutions. Drawing on the legendary histories of Doi Ang Salung Chiang Dao, Doi Suthep, and Doi Kham, the second chapter explores the various ways in which mountains in northern Thailand are constituted as a sacred space and, therefore, as an environment to be respected rather than exploited. The stories of these three sacred sites are told in chapters three and four as narrated in traditional northern Thai accounts called *tamnan* that I have chosen to translate as "legendary chronicle."

For my research on sacred mountain traditions in Southeast Asia beginning in 1994, I wish to acknowledge support from the Simon E. Guggenheim Foundation, the Fulbright-Hayes Program, the National Endowment for the Humanities, and Swarthmore College. Susan Offner of Silkworm Books helped in the final editing. Nancy C. Swearer's keen editorial eye and tireless effort greatly improved the book through its several drafts. Finally, the contributions to this volume by Sommai Premchit, my friend and collaborator for many years, and Phaithoon Dokbuakaew were immeasurable and deserving of coauthorship. Draft translations of *Tamnan Ang Salung*, begun in 1994 (Phaithoon and Swearer), and of *Tamnan Phra That Doi Suthep*, begun in 1999 (Sommai and Swearer), were completed in the spring of 2002, together with the legend of Phra That Doi Kham and Chao Luang Kham Daeng (Swearer). I am the sole author of chapters one and two and the introductions to chapters three and four.

A note on transliteration and transcription: common nouns in Thai and Pali generally follow the rules of the Royal Institute of Thailand which does not use diacritical marks. Proper nouns are usually transcribed as they are pronounced in Thai but in some cases follow their Pali orthography. For example, Chamathewi rather than Camadevi, Hariphunchai rather than Haripuñjaya, but nirvana rather than *nipphan* or nibbana, and dharma rather than *tham* or dhamma. The generic term for deities follows the Thai pronunciation, *thewada*, rather than *devata*, but classifications of supernatural beings are treated as proper nouns and follow Pali orthography, and are capitalized rather than italicized, e.g. Naga (serpent) rather than Nak, Yakkha (demon) rather than Yak.

Donald K. Swearer
Chiang Mai, 2004

CHAPTER I

BUDDHISM, NATURE, AND CULTURE

INTRODUCTION: RELIGION AND THE GLOBAL ENVIRONMENTAL CRISIS

The global environmental crisis has provoked heated debate in the scientific, government, and public policy sectors. Unfortunately, this debate has largely ignored the humanistic, ethical, and religious dimensions of the crisis. This ignorance stems from a utilitarian, cost-benefit philosophy ill equipped to challenge the basic assumptions undergirding an economic model of ever-expanding growth and consumption. If the dominant paradigm of economic growth and development is to be questioned, then ethical values and principles must be at the forefront of the environmental debate. The ethical factor contests the strategy of governments and corporations that continue business as usual under the pretext of inconclusive scientific data regarding the human causes of global warming, for example, not by taking sides on the scientific debate but by challenging the very premise of unbridled growth and consumption. In short, the qualitative question, "What is the good life?" challenges the usual quantitative answer to that question. Ethical and religious perspectives on the environmental crisis do not naively overlook its very real and important scientific, economic, and political policy aspects; however, without these perspectives we run the risk of ignoring the fact that global environmental problems raise fundamental questions about the intrinsic relationship of humans to nature and the related issue of distributive justice between rich and poor nations.

The world's religious and spiritual traditions contribute crucial dimensions to the environmental agenda: ideals of human flourishing,

I

holistic cosmologies, and moral imperatives. Religionists, both adherents and scholars, who are concerned about the environmental crisis have found in religious traditions resources that both focus and broaden its ethical dimensions. Religious scriptures, doctrines, and practices are being invoked to promote a holistic, non-anthropocentric, egalitarian, eco-friendly worldview respectful of nature and compassionate to all forms of life. Buddhists cite the compatibility between the Buddhist worldview of interdependent co-arising and an environmentally sustainable way of living in the world, the values of compassion and nonviolence, and the model of a minimalist lifestyle exemplified by the Buddha and the early monkhood (*sangha*) as critical contributions to the dialogue on ways to live in an increasingly crowded, polluted, and threatened world. Economic globalization accompanied by rapid social and cultural transformation, the dramatic depletion of the world's natural resources, and the frightening reality of global climate change form the backdrop to a Buddhist environmental ethic.

During the past half-century economic and social configurations have changed dramatically throughout the world due to population increases, urbanization, industrialization, and technological development. To a certain extent, these changes have created a common economic culture determined by the necessities of the modern nation state and the global market of multinational corporations. This economic culture is primarily materialistic, defining human well-being in terms of the production and consumption of goods, and measuring the wealth of a nation primarily in terms of its GNP (Gross National Product) rather than more illusive qualitative measurements of human happiness. The very concept of "development" is couched almost exclusively in material terms.

The emergence of an economically defined modern culture has led to a general increase in life expectancy among many populations of the world as housing and health services, for example, have improved. With respect to material aspects of life, more people share in the benefits of the increased production and use of various kinds of goods. Yet, even from an economic perspective the increase in the production and use of goods has been a mixed blessing. Even though by GNP measurements the world has seen a significant increase in the amount of material wealth, critics are quick to point out the increasing disparity between the rich and the poor in both developing and developed countries. For instance, in Thailand since the 1980s conflicts over water use between the wealthier industrial-urban sector and the poorer agricultural-farming sector have prompted numerous farmer protests over low water supplies that came to a head in the drought year of 1993.[1]

Globally, despite improvements in agricultural technology, hunger continues to be a persistent and pervasive problem. Furthermore, the capital intensive green revolution of an earlier generation dependent on chemical fertilizers and pesticides created as many systemic, long range problems as it solved, and current biotechnological research is raising even more questions regarding the consequences of genetic engineering.[2]

Although developments in many different kinds of technologies have led to dramatic breakthroughs in everything from space exploration to microscopic laser surgery, at the same time they have contributed to a sense of hopelessness and violence suffered by modern society in the form of the plague of drug addiction, the pervasive threat of terrorism and armed conflict, and the seemingly intractable problem of toxic waste disposal and the widespread contamination of water and food supplies. This modern economic culture has also had a generally deleterious effect on classical moral values and religious worldviews, and on traditional ways of understanding human existence and what constitute happiness and the good. In recent years the news media in Thailand has devoted considerable attention to the conflicts between the goals of national and commercial development, the well-being of the majority of the Thai people (especially the rural, farming populations), and the health of the environment. Dr. Anan Kanchanapan of the Faculty of the Social Sciences at Chiang Mai University observes that development in Thailand has emphasized the GNP and in doing so has undermined the moral and spiritual integration between the social and natural environment.[3] An article in the *Matichon* newspaper charged that development in Thailand has benefitted the urban elites at the expense of the environment, and proposed a reformist Buddhist perspective that would challenge selfishness and greed and the excessive lifestyle that has resulted from "too much wealth, too much power, too much to eat and drink, too many cars and mistresses."[4]

3

In the face of a perceived threat to traditional ways of life by modern economic culture, some seek a return to the fundamental verities of a simpler era believed to be embodied in an earlier historical age or represented by an idealized, mythic time of primal beginnings. Religious fundamentalisms, whether Christian, Jewish, Muslim, Hindu, or Buddhist, may be interpreted as a retreat from the confusions and threats of the modern world to the simple truths and values of an earlier age. But there are other, more creative and constructive religious responses to modernity than today's various fundamentalisms. Thoughtful religious adherents throughout the world are seeking to understand and interpret their traditions in ways that preserve the lasting insights and values of their faith, while at the same time engaging the realities of existence in today's violent world rather than retreating from them. One arena of engagement is the global environmental crisis.

BUDDHIST ENVIRONMENTALISM

In responding to the global environmental crisis abetted by the increasing commodification of values, Buddhists find in their worldview of causal interdependence a principle that integrates all aspects of life on four levels: existential, moral, cosmological, and ontological. Existentially, Buddhists affirm that all sentient beings share the fundamental conditions of birth, old age, suffering, and death. The existential realization of the universality of suffering lies at the core of the Buddha's teaching. Insight into the nature of suffering, its cause, cessation, and the path to the cessation of suffering became the essence of the Buddha's enlightenment experience. This quadratic teaching forms the basis of the four noble truths, the Buddha's first public teaching. The tradition conveys this universal truth via the narrative of the founder's path to nirvana and the logic of the four noble truths, but also in many other stories. In one, the Buddha is approached by a young mother after the death of her infant child. She pleads with the Blessed One to restore the life of her child. The Buddha responds by asking the grieving mother to bring a mustard seed from a house in the village where death had never entered, and that if she finds such a seed he will restore her child's life. The mother returns to the Buddha not with the mustard seed but with the realization of the universality of suffering caused by death.

Buddhism links the existential condition of the universality of suffering with the moral virtue of compassion. After his awakening to the cause and cessation of suffering, the Buddha decides to share his knowledge and the path to the cessation of suffering rather than selfishly keeping this insight to himself. This is regarded by the tradition as an act of universal compassion. Buddhist environmentalists assert that the mindful awareness of the universality of suffering produces compassionate empathy for all forms of life, particularly for all sentient species. They interpret the Buddhist ethical injunction to refrain from evil and to do good as a moral principle advocating the nonviolent alleviation of suffering, an ideal embodied in the prayer of universal loving-kindness that concludes many Buddhist rituals: "May all beings be free from enmity; may all beings be free from injury; may all beings be free from suffering; may all beings be happy." Out of a concern for the entire living environment, Buddhist environmentalists extend loving-kindness, compassion, and respect beyond people and animals to include plants and the earth itself.

The concepts of karma and rebirth integrate the existential sense of a shared common condition of all sentient life forms with the moral dimension of the Buddhist cosmology. Not unlike the biological sciences, rebirth links human and animal species. Evolution maps commonalties and differences among species on the basis of physical and genetic traits. Rebirth maps them in moral terms. Every form of sentient life participates in a karmic continuum traditionally divided into three world-levels and a hierarchy of five or six life forms. Differences among life forms and individuals are relative, however, not absolute. All forms of karmically conditioned life—human, animal, divine, demonic—are related within contingent, cyclical time: "In the long course of rebirth there is not one among living beings with form who has not been mother, father, brother, sister, son, or daughter, or some other relative. Being connected with the process of taking birth, one is kin to all wild and domestic animals, birds, and beings born from the womb (*Lankavatara Sutra*). Nirvana, the Buddhist *summum bonum*, offers the promise of transforming karmic conditionedness into an unconditioned state of spiritual liberation, a realization potentially available to all forms of sentient life on the

5

karmic continuum. That plants and trees or the land itself have a similar potential for spiritual liberation became an explicit doctrine in Chinese and Japanese Buddhism but may even have existed as part of popular Buddhist belief from earliest times—in sum, a realization that all life forms share both a common problematic and promise: "*bodhisattvas* each of these, I call the large trees" (*Lotus Sutra*).

The Buddha's insight into the cause of suffering and the path to its cessation is not merely personal in nature but cosmological. Tradition records that during the night of this defining experience the Blessed One first recalls his previous lives within the karmic continuum; then he perceives the fate of all sentient beings within the cosmic hierarchy; finally he fathoms the nature of suffering and the path to its cessation formulated as the Four Noble Truths and the law of interdependent co-arising. The Buddha's enlightenment unfolds in a specific sequence: from an understanding of the *particular* (his personal karmic history), to the *general* (the karmic history of humankind), and finally to the *principle* underlying the cause and cessation of suffering. Subsequently, this principle is further generalized as a *universal law of causality*: "on the arising of this, that arises; on the cessation of this, that ceases." Buddhist environmentalists find in the principle of causal interdependence a vision that integrates all aspects of the cosmology or ecosphere—particular individuals and general species—in terms of the principle of mutual co-dependence. The three stages of the Buddha's enlightenment experience can also be seen as representing a model for moral reasoning applicable to environmental ethics that integrates general principles (*e.g.*, interdependence), collective action guides (*e.g.*, non-killing), and the application by individual moral agents of principles and action guides in particular contexts.

In the Buddhist cosmological model individuals are by their very nature relational, thereby undermining the autonomous self over against the "other" whether human, animal, or vegetable. Buddhist environmentalists regard their worldview as a rejection of hierarchical dominance of one human over another or humans over nature, and as the basis of an ethic of empathetic compassion that respects bio-diversity. This view is echoed by the noted twentieth-century Thai Buddhist monk, Buddhadasa Bhikkhu,

The entire cosmos is a cooperative. The sun, the moon, and the stars live together as a cooperative. The same is true for humans and animals, trees and the earth. Our bodily parts function as a cooperative. When we realize that the world is a mutual, interdependent, cooperative enterprise, that human beings are all mutual friends in the process of birth, old age, suffering, and death, then we can build a noble, even a heavenly environment. If our lives are not based on this truth then we'll all perish.[5]

In Mahayana teachings the cosmological vision of interdependent causality evolved into a more substantive sense of ontological unity. Metaphorically, the Hua-yen (Japanese, Kegon) image of Indra's net of interconnected jewels each reflecting all the others has been especially important in Buddhist ecological discussions: "Just as the nature of earth is one while beings each live separately, and the earth has no thought of oneness or difference, so is the truth of all the Buddhas." For the American poet Gary Snyder, the Hua-yen image of the universe as a vast net of many-sided jewels each comprised by the reflections of all the other jewels with each jewel being the image of the entire universe, symbolizes the world as a universe of bio-regional ecological communities.

BUDDHISM AND AN ECOLOGY OF HUMAN FLOURISHING

Even though the image of the Buddha seated under the tree of enlightenment traditionally was not interpreted as a paradigm for ecological discourse, today's Buddhist environmental activists emphasize that the decisive events in the Buddha's life occurred in natural settings, in particular that the Buddha Gotama was born, attained enlightenment, and died under trees. The textual record, furthermore, testifies to the importance of forests, as a preferred environment for spiritual practices such as meditation as well as a place where laity sought instruction. Historically in Asia and increasingly in the West, Buddhists have situated centers of practice and teaching in forests and among mountains at some remove from the distractions of urban life. A model of simple living within a natural setting can be found in the Buddha's life.

In the Sutta on the Noble Search (*Ariyapariyesana Sutta, Majjhima Nikaya*, 26) the Buddha describes his quest for enlightenment (nirvana). In his search for the "supreme state of sublime peace" he first became a student of the noted religious teacher, Alara Kalama. He soon mastered Alara's teaching but found that it did not lead to dispassion, peace, or the direct knowledge of enlightenment so he sought out another famous spiritual leader of the day, Uddaka Ramaputta. The future Buddha proved so adept a pupil that Uddaka invited him to lead his community. Although Uddaka's teaching transported the future Buddha to a sublime state of consciousness beyond neither-perception-nor-non-perception, it, too, failed to satisfy the future Buddha's search for the good, so:

> Seeking the supreme state of sublime peace, I wandered by stages through the Magadhan country until eventually I arrived at the Senanigama near Uruvela. There I saw a delightful stretch of land and a lovely woodland grove, and a clear flowing river with a delightful forest so I sat down there thinking, 'Indeed, this is an appropriate place to strive for the ultimate realization of that unborn supreme security from bondage, Nirvana.'

According to The Sutta of the Noble Search, such a natural setting provides the ideal conditions for the relinquishing of attachment, the destruction of craving, and the attainment of the state of equanimity and dispassion requisite to perceive the truth of the interdependent, co-arising nature of things. What a contrast to the shopping malls of today's globalized economy designed to promote attachment, craving, and acquisitive passion!

Buddhadasa Bhikkhu regarded Wat Suan Mokh, his forest monastery in Chaiya, south Thailand, in terms reminiscent of The Noble Search. In naming his monastery the Garden of Empowering Liberation, he observed,

> Trees, rocks, sand, even dirt and insects can speak. This doesn't mean, as some people believe that they are spirits (*phi*) or deities (*thewada*). Rather, if we reside in nature near trees and rocks we'll discover feelings and thoughts arising that are truly out of the ordinary. At first we'll feel a sense of peace and serenity which may eventually move beyond that feeling to a transcendence of self. The deep sense of calm

that nature provides through separation [*wiwek*] from the troubles and anxieties which plague us in the day-to-day world functions to protect heart and mind. Indeed, the lessons nature teaches us lead to a new birth beyond the suffering that results from attachment to self. Trees and rocks, then, can talk to us. They help us understand what it means to cool down from the heat of our confusion, despair, anxiety, and suffering."[6]

Buddhadasa discovered the deepest truths about the dharma—the principles governing reality—in nature: "If we don't spend time in places like this [Wat Suan Mokh], it will be virtually impossible for us to experience peace and quiet. It is only by being in nature that the trees, rocks, earth, sand, animals, birds, and insects can teach us the lesson of self-forgetting."[7] In Buddhadasa's spiritual bio-centric view, being attuned to the lessons of nature is tantamount to being one with the dharma. By inference, the destruction of nature implies the destruction of the dharma. Toward the end of Buddhadasa's life the degradation of the natural environment became a deep concern. One of his talks at Wat Suan Mokh in 1990, three years before his death, was titled, "Buddhists and the Care of Nature" [*Phutthasasanik Kap Kan Anurak Thammachat*]. The concept of caring for nature stands at the heart of Buddhadasa's environmental ethic.

Only in relatively recent years has it become widely accepted that the destruction of the Brazilian rain forest, the ocean dumping of toxic waste, and the global increase in carbon dioxide levels affect the entire world's ecosystem, and that, on a personal level, whether or not I conserve water, electricity, and gasoline affects the health of the entire cosmos as well as my budget. To care for nature, therefore, stems from a realization that I do not and cannot exist independently of my total environment. I am not an island unto myself, or, in Buddhadasa's terminology, I do not and cannot exist unto myself because to do so contravenes the very laws of nature.

In Buddhadasa's view, that each person's well-being inextricably depends on the well-being of everything and everyone else and vice versa, is an indisputable, absolute truth. "The deep sense of calm that nature provides through separation from the stress that plagues us in the day-to-day world protects our heart and mind. The lessons nature teaches us lead to a new birth beyond suffering caused by our acquisitive self-centeredness." To act contrary to this truth is to suffer the consequences. In Buddhadasa's dramatic terms "the greedy and selfish are destroying nature....Our whole environment has been poisoned—prisons everywhere, hospitals filled with the physically ill, and we can't build enough facilities to take care of all the mentally ill. This is the consequence of utter selfishness....And in the face of all of this our greed and selfishness continues to increase. Is there no end to this madness?"[8]

Buddhadasa did not intend for the Garden of Empowering Liberation to be a retreat from the world but a place where all forms of life—humans, animals, and plants—can live as a cooperative microcosm of a larger ecosystem and as a community where humans can practice an ecological ethic. Such an ethic highlights the virtues of restraint, simplicity, loving-kindness, compassion, equanimity, patience, wisdom, nonviolence, and generosity. These virtues represent moral ideals for all members of the Buddhist community—monk, lay person, political leader, ordinary citizen, male, female. Political leaders who have the mandate to maintain the peace and security of the nation are admonished to adhere to the Buddhist principle of nonviolence. The Buddhist ethic of distributive justice extols the merchant who generously provides for the needy. Even ordinary Thai rice farmers traditionally left a portion of rice unharvested in their fields for the benefit of the poor and for hungry herbivores. For contemporary international Buddhist leaders such as the Dalai Lama, a sense of responsibility rooted in compassion lies at the very heart of an ecological ethic: "The world grows smaller and smaller, more and more interdependent...today more than ever before life must be characterized by a sense of universal responsibility, not only...human to human but also human to other forms of life."[9]

For Buddhist enviromentalists, Buddhadasa's Garden of Empowering Liberation provides an example of a sustainable lifestyle grounded in the values of moderation, simplicity, and non-acquisitiveness. We cannot rely on technology alone to solve the ecocrisis. Rather the solution to the crisis demands a transformation of values and lifestyle that I have termed, "an ecology of human flourishing." Buddhadasa's vision for the Garden of Empowering Liberation brings an ethical and spiritual critique to bear upon the confidence that science and technology can solve the global environmental crisis without taking into account the more profound spiritual and moral issues at the heart of human flourishing and true happiness.

Entrance to Chiang Dao cave

Buddha images at the entrance to Chiang Dao cave

Chedi enshrining relics of Luang Pu Sim, Wat Pha Plong, Doi Ang Salung Chiang Dao

Cave sanctuary, Wat Pha Plong, Doi Ang Salung Chiang Dao

Naga-guarded staircase ascending to Wat Phra That Doi Suthep

Pilgrims circumambulating chedi, Wat Phra That Doi Suthep

Chedi, Wat Phra That Doi Suthep

Pilgrims paying respects, Wat Phra That Doi Suthep

View of the Chiang Mai valley from Wat Phra That Doi Kham

Chedi, Wat Phra That Doi Kham

Chamathewi, Wat Phra That Doi Kham

Buffalo sacrifice propitiating the Lawa guardian spirits of Doi Kham and Doi Suthep, Ban Hiya, Doi Kham, 1994

Spirit medium, Chao Luang Kham Daeng shrine, Ban Mae Na, Chiang Dao, 2002

MOUNTAINS
AND SACRED SPACE

INTRODUCTION

The texts, doctrines, and practices that inform a holistic ecological worldview and vision of human flourishing are essential to a Buddhist environmental ethic; however, the specific cultural and environmental contexts that inform Buddhist traditions play an equally if not more important role. In northern Thailand, for example, Buddhism combined with various religious, cultural, and environmental variables to fashion a picture of a meaning-filled life within the physical terrain known as Lan Na, the Land of a Million Rice Paddies. In particular, these variables fused together with Buddhism to form a unified story that integrates the culture of the city with nature. Given the topography of northern Thailand, it is not surprising that mountains are a central feature of these narratives. In addition to being the focal point of legend, they are prime locations for monasteries, temples, and *ashrams*. Consequently, they are sought out by pilgrims, yogis, and meditators as an ideal environment for religious practice and devotion. Mountains embody awesome power. They simultaneously harbor the primordial guardians of the land and symbolize the axis of both cosmology and the state. For this reason, mountains also figure into Buddhist conceptions of kingship.

The following diagram offers a schematic picture of northern Thai sacred mountain topography as a natural phenomenon and a work of culture. At the center of the diagram is the mountain itself. In the case of Doi Ang Salung Chiang Dao, extensive limestone caves enhance the sense of the mountain's mystical sacrality. Mountains conjoined with caves together figure prominently in Buddhist symbolic and cosmological schemes. The mountain as a topographic feature of

COSMOLOGY

TOPOLOGY/ NATURAL ENVIRONMENT

Sacred Mountains in Northern Thailand

a landscape inspires awe, respect, fear, curiosity, and reverence. Its height serves as a point of spacial orientation and the axial center of a cosmological worldview associated with kingship. Imagined as the abode of autochthonous, Brahmanical, and Buddhist deities, spirits, and sacred beings, the mountain's wilderness environment serves as a magnet for spiritual virtuosi—shamans, ascetical monks, and hermits (*ruesi*)—as well as pilgrims who journey to the temples and monasteries located there. Both oral and written traditions codify the mythic, legendary, and historical significance of the mountain for present and future generations—at least until they fade from cultural memory.

The diagram features Buddhist elements—the Buddha made present through relic, image, and footprint, and a variety of Buddhist practitioners including ordinary monks or *bhikkhus* (Thai, *phra*), monks revered for their sacred charisma (*luang pu, khruba*), and lay pilgrims. Brahmanical elements are represented by Hindu ascetics or *ruesi* and numerous deities, or *thewada*, and gods, the most prominent in Buddhist legends being Indra. Guardian deities—Chao Luang Kham Daeng in the case of Doi Ang Salung Chiang Dao, and Pu Sae/Ya Sae in the case of Doi Suthep and Doi Kham—are ritually invoked not by monks or ascetics but through spirit mediums (*ma-khi* = horse that is ridden) and shamans. Through the enshrinement of relics on mountains in the case of Doi Suthep, kings not only serve as patrons of holy sites but also as agents by which mountains are sacralized. In this capacity the king is depicted as one who maintains the dharma through patronage and reigns as the lord of the cosmos (*chakkaphat*).

Culture, as human achievement or intellectual and artistic product, has been associated with urban civilization in opposition to nature, which is considered to be uninhabited or uncultivated space. When constructed in this way, "culture" and "nature" are seen in tension or opposition. However, when culture is perceived as a total way of life of a group of people, then nature becomes part of the way in which a people understand and construct their very existence. Over the centuries northern Thais have understood themselves not only in terms of cities (*mueang*) and cultivated land but also their relationship to wild nature, in particular the forested, mountain terrain that typifies the region. For instance, in the legend of the founding of the Mon kingdom of Hariphunchai (modern Lamphun) recounted in the *Chamathewiwong* (The Legend of Queen Chama), it is mountain hermits who bring Queen Chama from Lawo (modern Lopburi) to be Hariphunchai's first ruler and, consequently, the ascetics act as cultural mediators. Furthermore, although building the city meant clearing forested land and expelling indigenous inhabitants, the nearby mountains, especially Doi Suthep and Doi Kham, form an important part of the city's legendary history. In the legends of Doi

Suthep, Doi Kham, and Doi Ang Salung Chiang Dao, supernatural figures identified with the mountains become protectors of the inhabitants of the valleys. Even today, as an extension of the Thai new year (*songkran*) festivities in May, at the village of Mae Hiya at the base of Doi Kham, a buffalo is offered as a sacrifice to Pu Sae and Ya Sae, the guardian deities identified with Doi Suthep and Doi Kham. In April at a shrine in the village of Mae Na near Doi Ang Salung Chiang Dao, a medium invokes the spirit of Chao Luang Kham Daeng and his royal retainers from the mountain's cave to guarantee a prosperous rice harvest.

NARRATIVES OF PLACE: DOI ANG SALUNG

Stories of mountains and legendary figures, ascetics, and supernatural beings of various kinds including gods and demons, were perennial favorites in the rich folklore of northern Thailand. These oral legends with pre-Thai origins were in time written on palm leaves and thick mulberry paper albums that became part of the popular preaching traditions of northern Thai Buddhism, and in this process of amalgamation and subsequent transformation they were Buddhasized. The Buddha emerges as the dominant figure in the narratives. Everyone else, whether ordinary villagers, ascetics, monks, kings, or supernatural beings, all play their part to facilitate the Buddha's journey through the mountains and valleys of northern Thailand. The primary intent of these *tamnan* (chronicles/legendary histories) of the Buddha's journey throughout Lan Na is to establish northern Thailand as a sacred land—literally a Buddha-land (*Buddhadesa*)—through a legacy of signs, primarily bodily relics and footprints. Thus, the *Tamnan Ang Salung* (The Legend of Water Basin Mountain) situates the story of the mountain within the broader context of the Buddha's visit to northern Thailand and the sacralization of the land. The actual text appears to be a composite drawn from several distinct narratives, with only one focusing on the mountain itself.

Mountains bracket the *Tamnan Ang Salung* narrative. The Buddha's travels recounted in the text begin at Doi Kung, a small peak south of Chiang Mai proper, and end with an account of Doi Ang Salung Chiang Dao. Between these peaks the Buddha

Doi Ang Salung, Chiang Dao, shrouded by clouds

wanders throughout the Chiang Mai valley with occasional forays into the broader reaches of the extended and quasi-mythical space of Jambudipa. Although Jambudipa has a specific reference to the Indian subcontinent, in northern Thai *tamnan* it has a broader geographical and cosmological significance. Thus, the Buddha's itinerary links northern Thailand to the larger Buddhist world, a connection symbolized by the Buddha's physical relics widely distributed that are collected at Doi Ang Salung Chiang Dao and also at Doi Suthep, symbolizing an intensified concentration of the Buddha's powerful presence at these mountain sites.

During his travels throughout Lan Na the Buddha meets a variety of local inhabitants, particularly the Lawa, the pre-Mon and pre-Thai indigenous population of the area. Early in the narrative he visits a Lawa village situated at the foot of an unnamed mountain. Residing temporarily to the south of the village, the Buddha and the monks who accompany him are offered food by its inhabitants. After the Buddha and the monks have taken their meal, King Asoka— who, in total disregard of chronological and historical time, accompanies the Buddha on his travels—tells the Lawa that if they became the Buddha's followers they no longer will need to irrigate their fields

Aerial view of Doi Chiang Dao (Hans Penth 1976)

with a water wheel. After taking the precepts, the Lawa returned home and found that everything both inside and outside the house had turned to gold. Amazed, they exclaimed, "In the past we worked our fingers to the bone and still didn't have enough to eat. Now that we have taken the Buddha's precepts we find that everything has turned to gold. The Buddha's precepts are precious, indeed! We will observe them all of our lives."

As portrayed in the above example, in the belief system of the northern Thai, the actual presence of the Buddha assumes a magical aura. Even taking the five precepts (e.g., not to kill, not to lie) is glossed as prosperity and good luck rather than as strictly adhering to the ethical principles the precepts embody. Additionally, the Buddha's encounters also ascribe meaning to the places he visits as recorded by the acts of naming that take place throughout the text:

> After the Buddha had given the Lawa the precepts, he spoke to the monks: "Before I came here, the Lawa had to use a water wheel to irrigate their fields because this is a very dry area. Consequently, this place shall be known as Hot." The monks and King Asoka then said

to the Buddha, "O Blessed One, you should establish your religion (*sasana*) here. The Lawa will worship you by raising tall banners (*tung*)[1] in your honor. A large dwelling place will be constructed for you and your disciples, known as Jotikarama."[2]

This brief account of the Buddha's encounter with the Lawa provides an etiology for the name of the town of Hot, explains the use of traditional long banners at northern Thai and Shan festivals, and legitimates the founding of a monastery which may be a reference to Wat Suan Dok (The Flower Garden Monastery). Subsequently, the Buddha predicts that the kingdom of Chiang Mai will be established as a center for monks and scholars and that those who dwell there who do not attain nirvana during his lifetime will do so in the time of Phra Ariya Metteya, the future Buddha, who will usher in a new Buddhist era.

The Buddha continues his itinerary with little geographic regard by the compiler. Most of the sites are in the Chiang Mai region but towns in Burma and northern India are also included and predictions are made regarding the future rulers of Lan Chang (in Laos), Chiang Mai, and Hongsawadi (in Burma). The Blessed One bestows various signs of his presence—hair relics and footprints being the most prominent—and grants permission for the construction of Buddha images. In the *Tamnan Ang Salung* the Buddha's hair is the predominant relic. Other bodily relics are usually consigned to post-mortem predictions. Occasionally, however, physical parts of the Buddha other than hair become relics in rather startling ways as illustrated in the episode where the Buddha encounters a Lawa farmer who mistakes the Blessed One for a demon (Yakkha). Reassured that he was not a demon but the Lord Buddha, the farmer sits down beside him:

> As they were sitting under the tree, mucus dripped from the Buddha's nose but miraculously floated up to the leaves of the Asoka tree giving them a golden hue. Ananda collected the mucus- covered leaves and fashioned them into a relic which he gave to the Lawa farmer. Indra, who together with the monks and Visukamma had joined the Buddha and Ananda, made a pyramidal reliquary tower [to house the relic]. Afterwards, the Buddha spoke to them, "This relic will be here as long as you live. In the future it will be known as Chom Thong because the

relic was given to the farmer on the leaves of the Thong tree. This relic has the power to determine who is good and who is evil."[3]

Doi Ang Salung Chiang Dao is visited by the Buddha during his travels in northern Thailand and serves as an axial center from which the righteous world ruler will address the evils of the world which the text describes in great length as a time of war and suffering, malfeasance, immorality, and injustice, "...tradition and custom will disappear, and people will pursue their own selfish interests," and so on. The decline of Buddhism in the apocalyptic sections of the *Tamnan Ang Salung* refers to material representations of the Buddha, in this case, images and amulets, and sees commerce in such artifacts as a sign of the decline of the religion. A more momentous mark of the degeneration of the Buddhist age in the third millennium after the death of the Buddha, however, is the decline of the dharma and the *sangha* (monastic order). In this dark age (Kala Yuga), they are noted more by their absence than by their presence. As evidence for the decline of Buddhism the text notes:

> monks will not study the dharma; the laity will be lazy and interested only in eating and sleeping; and those who are illiterate and undisciplined will seek to escape responsible citizenship through ordination into the monkhood. People will be governed by greed and grasping; they will not seek either the way to heaven or to Nirvana and will enjoy doing only those things which lead to rebirth [*samsara*].

Doi Ang Salung Chiang Dao dominates the *tamnan*'s concluding section as a locus for signs of the Buddha after his death which, in turn, form part of a nexus for various sacred representations:

> When the Buddha had passed away at Kusinara, five hundred disciples took relics to Doi Aung Salung Chiang Dao. The Lord Indra, Brahma, the gods and demi-gods built a large golden *chedi* to a height of three hundred *wa* [six hundred meters] for the relics of the Buddha. The mountain was one *yot* [sixteen kilometers] high. A hermit lived there by the name of Brahmaruesi. Together with the gods Indra and Brahma, a Naga king named Virubakkha, and many deities, they fashioned a golden standing image of the Buddha two thousand meters high for both divine and human beings to worship. This precious image was

erected in the cave [of Chiang Dao]. Even those who see it from a distance and venerate the image make merit. Such an act guarantees them a long and successful life.

At this point a new character is introduced into the story, Chao Luang Kham Daeng, the guardian of Doi Ang Salung Chiang Dao and the surrounding area: "The ruler of the Yakkhas, Chao Luang Kham Daeng,[4] with ten thousand attendants guard the cave. In the cave are the possessions of divine beings and of kings, a priceless golden Bodhi tree, a golden Buddha image, and a golden *chedi* (reliquary). Chao Luang Kham Daeng and his attendants stand guard over these precious objects." The narrative then concludes with the following panegyric,

> Doi Ang Salung Chiang Dao is a place where the Buddha image, the Buddha relic, and relics of all the previous Buddhas, spiritually perfected (*arahant*) monks, and ascetics are kept. People who know [the importance of these objects] will care for the image and the relics. Everyone who knows this legend and who pays respects to the Buddha image and the relics of the Buddhas and the *arahant* monks at Doi Ang Salung, whether they come from far or near, will be blessed beyond calculation.[5]

Tamnan Ang Salung reveals the nature of the fifteenth-century worldview of northern Thai Buddhism that pertained up to the modern period. Even today many elements of that worldview are very much in evidence. In it the Buddha's presence operates in terms of three different yet related levels: magical, cosmological, and ontological. The first is the instrumental significance of a particular event or object; the second, the underlying meaning of the interrelationship among particular events and objects; the third, the overarching reference to which all events and objects point.

The first is the most obvious. In the episode at the Lawa village, for example, the benefit from observing the precepts is an abundance of riches. The same magical, instrumentalist view characterizes the installation and maintenance of bodily relics and Buddha images. These pious acts not only guarantee the survival of Buddhism, they bestow specific blessings on the patrons. In sum, contact with the Buddha, whether with his bodily person in the story's narrative present or as contact with the relics in the Buddha's absence, is the basis for the popular Buddhist understanding of blessing and merit.[6]

The second level of meaning points beyond a magical, instrumentalist view of particular events associated with the Buddha and his relics to the geographical and cosmological map in which they are imbedded. The Buddha's wanderings in northern Thailand constitute the region as the land of the Buddha. The presence of the Buddha literally gives the region an identity indicated by the giving of a name, a tradition associated with folklore.[7] As a consequence of the Buddha's visit, particular places are named and in doing so are given a location within the space created by the Buddha's itinerary.

The Buddha is the name giver, and in the act of naming he creates order. The Buddha's wanderings establish a map within which particular locations derive meaning as a result of being integrated into a larger scheme of things grounded ultimately in the Buddha. His visit to northern Thailand is a cosmogonic event that creates an ordered, meaningful world. The signs left by the Buddha, then, are not just reminders of his visit to Lan Na; rather, they are indicators of his continuing presence.

In the *Tamnan Ang Salung*, the cosmic center is Doi Ang Salung Chiang Dao, a point that integrates both time—past, present, and future—and space, the seemingly world-extended Jambudipa. Ang Salung Chiang Dao, as cave and mountain, brings together all the sacred signs of the Buddha—bodily relics, image, footprint, Bodhi tree; the powerful forces operative throughout the story—Asoka and other righteous world rulers, Indra, Brahma, and other superhuman forces; and the guardian hosts of the area—Chao Luang Kham Daeng and his retinue. The mountain's shape and looming presence give it a mysterious, *sui generis* power. However, the mountain's sacrality also depends on the legends associated with it and its place in the cultural traditions the northern Thais fashioned from Buddhism, Brahmanism, and indigenous animistic beliefs. The mountain, its stories, and beliefs linked to it continue to reinforce northern Thai identity through pilgrimage, as a favored site for Brahmanical and Buddhist asceticism, as the most revered location of northern Thai shamanism, and as a locus of patronage by the political and economic elites.

SACRED MOUNTAINS AND THEIR STORIES PAST AND PRESENT: DOI SUTHEP AND DOI KHAM

In 1994, I lived at the foot of Doi Suthep mountain in northern Thailand. Its summit of 1,601 meters (5,250 feet), overlooks Chiang Mai, Thailand's third largest city, a modern, bustling, increasingly crowded metropolis with a population exceeding three hundred thousand people. Everyday I viewed the mountain from my study window, observed it when I drove to my office at Chiang Mai University, and frequently visited the Buddhist temple near its summit. The face of the mountain constantly changed. In the months of March and April the parched hillsides were veiled in dust from the dry heat and residual smoke from seasonal burning. With the monsoon rains the mountain emerged from its brown haze with sharp, verdant clarity. By night the temple lights near its summit twinkled brightly like stars above the horizon and by day whispy white clouds often encircled the peak.

Doi Suthep became for me a virtual kaleidoscope of shapes, colors, and changing sights. The many faces that Doi Suthep showed me during the months I was her neighbor became a metaphor for my perception of sacred mountain traditions in northern Thailand. Just as physically a mountain is much more than a static, unchanging topographic feature on a map or a specific kind of geological formation, so also a mountain revered as "sacred" cannot be reduced to a single meaning or a single interpretation, even though a particular aspect of a sacred mountain may be foregrounded as is the case with Doi Suthep on whose summit resides Wat Phra That Doi Suthep, one of Thailand's most famous Buddhist monasteries and pilgrimage sites.

Reverence for Doi Suthep centers on Wat Phra That, to be sure, but includes much more. The mountain is considered as the auspicious guardian of the valley. Furthermore, the history of Buddhism in northern Thailand, the institutional relationship between Buddhism and kingship in Chiang Mai, the connection between the indigenous animism of the region and Buddhism, the formation of popular Buddhist devotional practices, and the revitalization of northern Thai Buddhist culture in the early twentieth century all center on the mountain. Doi Suthep looms large not only as a feature of the natural landscape but also in the

Wat Phra That Doi Suthep

landscape of the imagination, worldview, and history of the Tai Yuan of the Chiang Mai valley.

Mountains in the Doi Suthep Doi Pui range, especially Doi Suthep and Doi Kham, are the subject of northern Thai legend and myths. The valley's inhabitants are protected by the guardian spirits of the Lawa, Pu Sae/Ya Sae, who reside on the mountains and are placated and honored by an annual buffalo sacrifice. An ancient *chedi* on Doi Pui's summit is reputed to contain the remains of the Lawa chieftain, Wilangkha. According to legend, he was an unsuccessful suitor of Chamathewi (Camadevi) who ruled the Mon city of Hariphunchai (Haripunjaya) in the ninth century, four hundred years prior to the Tai subjugation of the area by King Mangrai. The mountain takes its name from the legendary hermit sage, Wasuthep (Vasudeva) identified as the son of Pu Sae/Ya Sae in some legends, a major figure who appears in other northern legends linked to the founding of Hariphunchai. In the legend of Doi Kham, Wasuthep becomes Chamathewi's guardian, and in other legends he arranges for her to come to northern Thailand from Lawo (modern Lopburi), as the first ruler of Hariphunchai. Today, devotees make offerings to Wasuthep's spirit at a shrine on the lower level of Wat Phra That

Doi Suthep and at a cave on the mountain's eastern slope where the ascetic is reputed to have lived.

Of surpassing historical and cultural significance, however, is Wat Phra That, the Buddhist temple-monastery near Doi Suthep's summit. Here myth and legend join to become history, and it is the historical legend of the enshrinement of the relic that dominates the *Tamnan Phra That Doi Suthep*. Tradition says that the sanctuary was established in the fourteenth century to house a Buddha relic brought by the monk, Sumana Thera, from the Thai kingdom of Sukhothai to Chiang Mai at the request of its ruler, Kue Na (1355–1385 C.E.), one of the great patrons of Buddhism in this northern kingdom. According to the Doi Suthep chronicle, after the relic arrived in Chiang Mai it miraculously divided itself. King Kue Na enshrined half the relic at the royal Flower Garden Monastery (Wat Suan Dok) located in Chiang Mai city. The other half was placed on the back of an elephant set loose to wander on the mountain in the belief that the animal would be led by the gods to a foreordained location, suggesting that supernatural forces determined the placement of the relic.

Other legends, included in the *tamnan*, tell a different story, one that connects Chamathewi, Wasuthep, and Doi Kham. These narratives illustrate the rich Lawa, Mon, and Thai cultural map that overlays Doi Suthep's imposing physical presence and around which the history of northern Thailand unfolds. As symbolic features, Doi Suthep, Doi Kham, and Doi Ang Salung Chiang Dao are prominent in the northern Thai cultural imagination and sense of identity, but have these mountains, once so rich with meaning, lost their power and significance, becoming mere tourist landscapes and spaces to be exploited commercially?

The contemporary significance of Doi Suthep as a sacred mountain and a work of culture became abundantly clear in 1986 during a controversy over the construction of an electric cable car from the base of the mountain to the monastery-temple, Wat Phra That, near the summit. The cable car, endorsed by the Tourist Authority of Thailand, would accommodate an ever-increasing number of tourists who flock to Thailand's northern mountains. Long gone are the days when pilgrimage to Wat Phra That was on foot, but the sealed two-lane road to the sanctuary built in 1934 with voluntary manual labor under the inspired leadership of the charismatic monk, Khruba Siwichai, has itself become part of the mountain's legendary history. However, the proposed cable car to be constructed by a commercial company to exploit Doi Suthep and promote the increasingly invasive commercial degradation of the mountain was another matter. Environmentalists, university professors, students, and ordinary citizens rose up in protest. A particularly key element in quashing the plan was the role played by Buddhist monks, notably the late Phothirangsi, then assistant ecclesiastical governor of the province of Chiang Mai and the highly respected abbot of Wat Phan Dong.[8] An abbreviated review of the defense of Doi Suthep in the face of the onslaught of commercial development and tourism is the following paragraph from Niranam Khorabhatham's editorial in the April 30, 1986, *Bangkok Post*, which illustrates the tenor of the rhetoric and the deep reverence for the mountain:

> The manager of the proposed cable car project on Doi Suthep, Chiang Mai, states that he was "not overlooking the sanctity of Wat Phra That." He underestimates the northern people: The Soul of Lanna [northern Thailand] is still alive. Northerners perceive, at least in their subconscious, that Mount Suthep is like a symbolic stupa. Doi Suthep's dome-like shape is like an immense replica of the ancient Sanchi style stupa, a gift to Lanna by the Powers of Creation. Stupas are reliquaries of saints. More than that, they are a structural representation of the very essence of Buddhism. Plant and animal life are like Nature's frescoes, both beautifying and exemplifying the Law [dharma] not less than paintings in any man-made shrine. Although sometimes not being able to explain why rationally, the northern people want to preserve the Stupa Doi Suthep as it was given to them by Creation, as untouched as possible, as sacred.

The pressures to exploit Doi Suthep for its tourist value threaten the mountain's natural environment and its cultural and religious integrity. The fact that Doi Suthep is perceived by northern Thais as a sacred landscape was a major factor in challenging and defeating both private and government plans to build a cable car to the top of the mountain and expand tourism and other commercial enterprises destructive to its natural environment. The reverence for Doi Suthep in the cultural imagination of northern Thais is unique, and the story of Doi Suthep from its legendary origin to today suggests that narratives of place are crucial in developing an environmental ethics. Indeed, when it comes to concrete action, as in the case of the cable car project, they can be decisive. Narratives that blend myth and history, past and present, give purpose and meaning to the lives of contemporary participants in an ongoing story.

In a unique way, the Doi Suthep cable car episode contextualizes the Buddhist principle of interdependence that forms the basis of a Buddhist environmental ethic. The stories of the Lawa chieftain, Wilangkha, the ascetic Wasuthep, and the miraculous Buddha relic enshrined at Wat Suan Dok and on the mountain illustrate the symbiotic interdependence between the mountain and the city. Whether one draws a relationship of tension between the two as symbolized by Wilangkha who was rejected by Queen Chama, or a relationship of collaboration as illustrated by Wasuthep, the mountain ascetic who founded the first city in northern Thailand, or a relationship of substantive unity as symbolized by the Buddha relic enshrined both in the city and on the mountain, the kingdoms of Hariphunchai and Chiang Mai derive their meaning not in isolation behind moated walls but in relationship to the mountain. Mountain and city are inextricably bound together and, as the narratives illustrate, their fates are mutually interdependent. This symbiosis depends on the fact that the mountain as a unique locus of the sacred, a spacial symbol of transcendence, is perceived as different from, yet essential to, the identity of the city.

In 1986 northern Thai Buddhists perceived the threat to Doi Suthep as a sacred mountain to be a menace to their own identity and well-being. If Doi Suthep and the mountains of northern Thailand degenerate into a terrain to be exploited for commercial value, more than trees and spectacular views will be lost; the morality and spiritual well-being—indeed, the very identity of a people—will be jeopardized as well. An environmental ethic depends on an understanding that our intrinsic nature as human beings is inextricably linked to nature, and that human flourishing depends on whether, in the words of Buddhadasa Bhikkhu, "we can listen to the voice of trees and mountains and hear the sound of the dharma."

CHAPTER III

DOI ANG SALUNG: WATER BASIN MOUNTAIN

INTRODUCTION

Doi Ang Salung, Water Basin Mountain, juts out like a molar tooth from the base of a small valley situated approximately sixty-five kilometers (forty miles) north of Chiang Mai. As early as the fourteenth century the area near the mountain may have served as a garrison town located between the early Tai city states of Fang and Chiang Mai founded by King Mangrai. Covering an area of about sixty square kilometers, the mountain's steep limestone slopes descend from a massif to a horseshoe-shaped valley surrounded by three peaks, the highest of which is about 2,186 meters (7,175 feet).

Thailand's third highest peak, Doi Ang Salung, most often called Doi Chiang Dao, the Mountain of the City of the Stars, is best known for its winding cave system running for over fourteen kilometers (8.5 miles) under the mountain. The height and size of the peak, its location, the nature and extent of its mysterious caves, and the sanctuary located in the cave's large antechamber give the mountain a special significance in the lore of northern Thailand. The mountain holds a unique position in the shamanistic traditions of northern Thailand, especially those that concern the major guardian spirit of the area, Chao Luang Kham Daeng. Ascetics and forest monks are drawn to the mountain, its caves, and the surrounding area as an ideal environment for the strenuous pursuit of higher spiritual realization. The renowned forest monk, Luang Pu Sim came to Chiang Dao in 1932 with Achan Man, the founder of the modern Thai forest tradition, and established a meditation retreat on the mountain's eastern slope. The sanctuary located in the cavernous chamber near the main cave's entrance is both a pilgrimage site and a popular tourist destination. Legendary tales of the Buddha's visit to northern Thailand include Doi Ang Salung, a narrative that contributes to the sacredness of the site.

Stories featuring Doi Ang Salung Chiang Dao were passed down orally and in the form of palm-leaf *tamnan*. The *tamnan* genre of northern Thai Buddhist texts is very extensive and includes a varied subject matter. In some cases the conventional meaning of chronicle as a historical account applies. As is often the case, however, the typical northern Thai *tamnan* is more appropriately considered a legend (*nithan*) rather than a historical account. The text translated in this chapter acknowledges this fact when the transcriber refers to the work as a *nithan*.

As monastery palm-leaf manuscript collections demonstrate, stories about the Buddha—his previous lives (*jataka*) and his visit to northern Thailand—were exceedingly popular in northern Thailand by the fourteenth and fifteenth centuries and continued to be written up to the early twentieth century. From the large numbers of these texts present in monastery collections, it appears that they were often given as donatory offerings and were preached regularly. The texts were written in the vernacular, in this case Tai Yuan, and even though interspersed with Pali terms and phrases, they were easily understood by northern Thai temple audiences.

Tamnan can be classified as folklore. The Legend of Water Basin Mountain incorporates many elements from the folklore of northern Thailand and specifically the Chiang Dao region, even though these folkloric aspects have been Buddhasized. The folklore incorporated into the text brings the traditional northern Thai worldview and cultural system to the fore. However, the text's folkloric aspect with its obscure references often pose difficulties for the translator.

The following rendering is based on a microfilm copy in the Social Research Institute archive, Chiang Mai University, of a palm-leaf manuscript in northern Thai that was found at the San Pa Khoi monastery of the municipal district of Chiang Mai. It was transcribed at a monastery in the district of Lamphun dated Culasakarat 1306 (1944 C.E.). The approximate date of the original text can only be surmised. Mention of Burmese monks suggests that it was written subsequent to Burmese suzerainty in northern Thailand sometime after 1558 C.E. A reference to King Kawila who ruled Chiang Mai from 1781 to 1813 C.E. is the strongest evidence for assigning a composition date for this version of the text to the early nineteenth century.

The manuscript appears to be a composite of three different stories: the Buddha's visit to northern Thailand, the decline of Buddhism in Jambudipa—which extends beyond India to include northern Thailand—two thousand years after the founding of Buddhism, and the story of the Chiang Dao mountain and cave. To make the text more readable I have rearranged paragraphs, abbreviated others, and introduced subheadings that do not appear in the palm-leaf manuscript. This serves to highlight the three different but related stories that comprise the text. Doi Ang Salung Chiang Dao links the three tales in the following ways: Chiang Dao is one of the sites visited by the Buddha; the cave-mountain is associated with the righteous ruler who will bring peace and order to the chaos of the declining world eon; and, finally, Chiang Dao possesses an inherent sacrality. The subheadings of the text are arranged as follows:

1. The Buddha's Journey among the Lawa, Tai, and Burmese. Relics, Footprints, and Buddha Images
2. The Apocalyptic Vision of the Dark Age (Kala Yuga). The Righteous Ruler
3. The Story of the Buddha's Journey Resumes
4. A Golden Deer and a White Rabbit Discuss the Future. The Apocalyptic Vision Continues
5. Doi Ang Salung Chiang Dao

The organization of the text highlighted by the subheadings suggests that the first and second stories originally were interspersed into the text. The story would be more coherent if section 3 followed section 1, and section 4 followed section 2. It could be, however, that the story of the golden deer and the white rabbit existed as an independent tale adapted from folklore to extend the discussion of the Buddhist apocalypse and the restorative role of a righteous ruler. It is interesting to note that the future Buddha, Phra Ariya Metteya (Mettrai) who is omnipresent in so many non-canonical Theravada apocalyptic and millenarian texts, receives limited mention in this *tamnan*.[1]

Because Chao Luang Kham Daeng figures so prominently in the legendary history of Doi Ang Salung Chiang Dao, a brief account of his transfiguration from a prince of the kingdom of Champa (Phayao) into a guardian Yakkha of the cave-mountain has been appended. This translation is based on a section of the narrative found in Sanguan Likhsit, *Tamnan Tham Luang Chiang Dao* (1972), a printed booklet sold at the site. The most recent account by Phramahasathit Tikkhayano was published in 2002 and is available in Thai and an awkward English translation.

TAMNAN DOI ANG SALUNG. THE LEGEND OF WATER BASIN MOUNTAIN [2]

The Buddha's Journey among the Lawa, Tai, and Burmese. Relics, Footprints, and Images

After the Buddha spent seven days at Doi Kung[3] he came down from the mountain and journeyed north through a forest for a distance of approximately 20,000 meters[4] to the Mae Ping River. There he met a Lawa[5] farmer who was using a water wheel to irrigate a field. When he saw the Buddha approach, the farmer unwound the turban from his head in order to wash the Buddha's feet. After he removed the turban from his head, it miraculously turned into gold. Amazed, the farmer said to the Buddha, "O, Blessed One, by your kindness please reside here in the north with us."

The Buddha acceded to this request and stayed at a mountain to the south of the Lawa village. The Lawa farmers offered the Buddha two pots of rice curry. After the Buddha had eaten, the *arahant* monks who accompanied him consumed the remainder of the meal.[6] When the Buddha and his disciples had finished eating, King Asoka, the righteous ruler, spoke to the Lawa:[7] "My dear Lawa, there's no longer any need for you to irrigate your fields with a water wheel. If you take the precepts of the Buddha, there will be sufficient food for you to eat." The Lawa then took the five precepts from the Buddha.[8] Upon returning to their home they found that everything had turned into gold. Amazed, they exclaimed, "In the past we worked our fingers to the bone and still didn't have enough to eat. Now that we have taken the Buddha's precepts we have found that everything has turned into gold. The Buddha's precepts are precious, indeed! We will observe them all of our lives."[9]

Aerial view of Chiang Dao city (Hans Penth 1976)

After the Buddha had given the Lawa the precepts, he spoke to the monks: "Before the Tathagata[10] came here the Lawa had to use a water wheel to irrigate their fields because this is a very dry area (Thai, *haeng hot*). Consequently, this place shall be known as Hot."[11] The *arahant* monks and King Asoka then said to the Buddha, "O Blessed One, you should establish your religion here. The Lawa will venerate you by raising tall banners in your honor, and elderly Burmese ascetics will burn their robes (*pha sabai*).[12] A large dwelling place will be constructed for you and your disciples, known as Jotikarama."[13] The *arahant* monks and King Asoka then took a hair relic from the Buddha, encased it in a container of bamboo, and enshrined it in a gilded container seven hands high. After putting the relic in a hole in the earth seven cubits (*sok*) deep,[14] they paid respect to it. Indra placed a spear in the ground at the site to protect it; the hole was covered up, and over it a *chedi* three hundred cubits high was constructed.[15] The Buddha then spoke to the monks and King Asoka, "After the Tathagata has passed away, my right hand bone relic will also be enshrined in this *chedi*."

The Buddha then proceeded to the home of a wealthy potter. There he preached a sermon on the meritorious blessing of building a monastic dwelling place and also of constructing Buddha images. The wealthy potter who had listened to the sermon decided then and there to construct Buddha images so he ordered his neighbors and the Lawa (Tamila)[16] to bring all the things needed to make 3,300,000 images.[17] [After they were made] the images were put on a high altar and everyone worshipped the Buddha. The Lawa, led by the wealthy merchant, then consecrated the images and worshipped them. The Buddha blessed the people saying, "Satthu...It is good that you have made these images of me because I cannot always be here with you.[18] After I have passed away this place will become a great city (i.e. Chiang Mai) where my religion will flourish. It will be a major center for monks and scholars. The officials of the kingdom as well as the common people will enjoy great good fortune and prosper in my religion. Those who live here but who do not reach nirvana in my lifetime will do so in the lifetime of the future Buddha, Phra Ariya Metteya." Afterwards, King Asoka and the monks buried the 3,300,000 Buddha images in the hole seven cubits deep. The Buddha looked into the future and made the following prediction, "When I have passed away, these images will appear before both divine and human beings so that they may be worshipped in this city now and in the future."

[After the Buddha images had been made and consecrated], the Buddha, the monks, and King Asoka walked up to the top of the mountain where the Blessed One offered a hair relic to ensure that his religion would be established there. The monks and King Asoka then put the hair relic in a bamboo container eight hands high and buried it in a hole one hundred cubits deep. Indra implanted a spear in the earth to protect the relic, and the Buddha announced that in the future that place would be known as " where the Buddha sat and slept" (*nang non*). [Following the installation of the hair relic at Doi Nangnon] the Lord Buddha journeyed to the town of Yom which [he blessed] with a footprint.[19] He [consecrated] the town of Fang [north of Chiang Mai] in a similar manner, and continued his journey though the towns of Chae and Takong (Rangoon) [in Burma], and Kusinara [in northwestern India]. Wherever he went people sought to become his disciples until there was a following of five hundred monks. Arriving at the Jetavanarama,[20] the Lord Buddha spent the rains retreat there. Twenty-five years after his enlightenment at the age of sixty the Lord Buddha had both placed and predicted the appearance of many relics and footprints throughout the area [of his travels].

The Lord Buddha, supreme among human and divine beings, was staying at the Jetavanarama when he reached eighty years of age.[21] Foreseeing that the end of his life was drawing near, the Tathagata traveled to the Tamila [Lawa] town of Fang[22] where, because of his past *karma*, he ate [tainted] pork and became ill. The Lord Buddha then said, "O friends, the time has come for my final nirvana."

The Lord Buddha, accompanied by Ananda Mahathera, King Asoka, Lord Indra, and the god Vissukamma walked to a deep, wide inlet at the edge of a large body of water. A large hardwood tree eight meters and two cubits tall grew along the bank. A flamingo flew near the Lord Buddha, pecked at him, and then landed on the tree. Afterwards a monkey appeared and grabbed at the Buddha before the monkey climbed into the tree. These two were followed by a white bird pecking for food on the ground and a pink, two-tongued turkey buzzard, both of whom flew to the tree. The Blessed One stood near the bank, smiled, and laughed quietly. Ananda Mahathera respectfully asked the Lord Buddha, "O Blessed One, why are you laughing?" The Lord Buddha answered him, "O beloved Ananda, after I have reached my final nirvana, this inlet will dry up and a great city will be built here known as Lan Chang Ayodhaya. The flamingo, the white bird, the turkey buzzard, and the monkey all will be reborn as kings [of Lan Chang]. They will be very powerful and will conquer many towns, both large and small. The king, his officials, and the citizens of the city will be deceitful (literally, "many tongued") like the two-tongued turkey buzzard. Like the white bird pecking for food which it carries away in its beak, the ministers on the right and the ministers on the left along with the king's soldiers will attack and plunder neighboring towns, stealing their cultural wealth without any compassion whatsoever. Like the actions of the flamingo and monkey, the behavior of the king, his ministers, and the citizens of Lan Chang will impede the progress of the Tathagata's religion."[23]

After the Lord Buddha made this prediction, he journeyed north with the *arahant* monks and Indra until they reached the bank of the Ping River. Walking along the river bank they came to another large inlet. Seeing the Buddha approaching from a distance, the Naga king who lived there was entranced. Having nothing to offer the Lord Buddha except a honeycomb from a tree by the bank, the Naga assumed the form of a human being, climbed the tree, carried the honeycomb down, and offered it to the Buddha. After accepting the Naga's offering of honey, the Buddha then rested on a pallet prepared by Ananda near the edge of the forest.

[Seated respectfully beside the Buddha] the Naga made the following request, "O Blessed One, please establish a footprint here, "to which request the Buddha replied, "Since there's no suitable flat stone for my footprint, I grant you permission to make a Buddha image. It will be known as the reclining Buddha of the honey inlet (*phra non nong phueng*) in remembrance of the gift of honey given to me by the Naga king.[24] To build, repair, or venerate this Buddha image will be the same as venerating the Tathagata when he was alive." Overjoyed, the Naga king made a reclining image of the Tathagata for both human and divine beings to venerate in the future.

After the Buddha made this prediction, he arose from his pallet and accompanied by the monks walked until it was nearly twilight. Seeing a Lawa farmer working in his paddy field plowing rice and noticing that he had no water [to irrigate his field], the Blessed One asked, "O lay devotee, what are you doing?" Startled and mistakenly taking the Buddha to be a demon, the farmer trembled with fright. "O lay disciple," the Blessed One assured him, "don't be afraid. I am a fully enlightened Buddha." When the farmer realized that the person standing before him was not a demon but the Lord Buddha, the farmer respectfully knelt to the ground and the Blessed One asked him if the monks could spend the night in his rice field. [Distressed at the prospect of the Lord Buddha sleeping on the bare ground] the farmer replied, "There's no need to sleep outside in the field, please stay in my hut which is nearby." When the Buddha answered that he would rather sleep on the bund of the rice paddy, the farmer prepared a bed of thatch for him. "O, Lord Buddha," he said, "please don't leave us in the morning before eating." At sunrise the Buddha honored the farmer's request and received food offerings from him.

[After the morning alms] Ananda requested a relic from the Buddha [to leave with the Lawa farmer]. Taking a hair from his head the Buddha gave it to Ananda who placed it in the hollow of a small bamboo container. Lord Indra then made a gilded lacquer box seven hands high to enshrine the relic. After digging a hole fourteen meters deep, he then placed the relic box in the hole and over it built a *chedi* seven cubits high.

The Lord Buddha instructed the farmer as follows: "[In the future] make a Buddha image and enshrine it on the bund of the rice paddy where I slept." [With downcast eyes] the farmer replied, "O Lord Buddha, I'm already an old man and am unable to comply with your request. Indra and Vissukamma then reassured the Lawa farmer, "Do not be discouraged. We will help you." And with that, Indra asked the Buddha when he wanted the image to be made. "Make the Buddha image one hundred years after I have passed away. If the people take care of the Buddha image and the relic, the village will prosper and the crops will be abundant, but if the people do not attend to the image and the relic, the village will decline and the fields will be infertile." Then the Buddha turned to Ananda and said, "Whoever makes and reveres a relic or an image will attain nirvana." "This image," the Buddha foretold, "will be called Phra Pan because the farmer made a channel from the river to irrigate his paddy field and on the bund a bed of dry thatch for me to sleep on. In the future this river will dry up."[25]

45

After the Buddha made this prediction he continued on toward the town of Fang. (If you want more details you should consult the *Buddha Nimitta*. In this text the Buddha visits northern Thailand three times and Fang only once.) At Fang the Buddha ate tainted pork at the home of Nai Chuntha. Experiencing acute pain the Buddha [left Fang] and went to stay in the cave at Mount Tap Tao.[26] That evening his followers (*sawok*)[27] summoned Dr. Komarapat. The doctor came and gave the Buddha some medicine, but the Blessed One vomited blood and showed no improvement. The doctor was bewildered. "When I administered this medicine in the past," he said, "it cured everyone to whom I gave it, both animals and humans. You must summon my teacher to help. He lives at Doi Duan at Phayao."[28]

Two of the Buddha disciples quickly departed for Phayao. Finding the sage at Mount Doi Duan they hastened to explain to him the Buddha's condition. He was irritated with Dr. Komarapat. "I'm already an old man. My hearing and sight are impaired and it's difficult for me to get up. Furthermore, I've given all of my treatment manuals to Dr. Komarapat." [Nevertheless, he agreed to go], so the two monks and the sage flew by their supernatural powers to the mouth of the cave at Mount Doi Tap Tao. Because he was such a very large man, the sage could not be carried inside so he knelt at the cave's entrance and the doctor came out to consult with his teacher. Depressions are still evident in the rock where the sage knelt. The sage requested that the Buddha's vomit be brought to him. Ananda gathered it and gave it to Phra Gavampati who, in turn, presented it to Doctor Komarapat who handed it to his teacher. After examining the Buddha's vomit the sage diagnosed tainted pork as the cause of the Buddha's illness.

"If we can't find medicine to counteract the poison of the spoiled pork, " he explained, "the Blessed One cannot be cured." The doctor asked one of the monks to fetch the medicine [at Mount Doi Duan.] Three times the monk returned with the wrong medicine so the ascetic went himself. (The Buddha foresaw that he would die and that therefore no medicine would cure him.) When he returned with the medicine, the ascetic gave it to Dr. Komarapat who passed it to Phra Gavampati, and then to Aniruddha, and finally to Ananda. When Ananda received the medicine a large opening miraculously appeared in the cave. The Buddha and Ananda walked through it to a stream at the base of a waterfall. A large flat stone the size of a preaching seat was located there. The Buddha sat on the stone seat while Ananda brought him some water [from the stream] to assuage his thirst. [After a short rest] the Blessed One told Ananda that he wanted to leave before Dr. Komarapat and the monks arrived.[29]

Departing from the waterfall they journeyed on to the cave at Chiang Dao mountain. They both entered the cave and after resting there a while went on their way. As they walked along they passed a large mango tree thirty hand spans high under which two white pigs were resting. The Buddha's illness forced him to lie down and rest. Ananda covered him carefully with a blanket. "O Ananda, I'm very thirsty," exclaimed the Buddha. Please get me some water from the Ping River over there and bring it to the Tathagata. I shall spend the night here under the mango tree."

Ananda took the Buddha's alms bowl to the river to fetch some water but while he was filling the bowl a Yakkha spied him there. Seeing Maha Ananda bending over to get water, the demon thought to himself, "I'll eat him," and grabbed both of Ananda's arms. Ananda looked at the demon and cried out, "I'm a disciple of the Buddha!" but the Yakkha merely replied, "That makes no difference to me. Vessavana [i.e., Kuvera] gave me the control of this area with permission to eat both two- and four-footed animals who pass by here if they can't tell me the godly meaning (*deva-dharma*) of the elements of earth and of water. If you are a disciple of the Buddha you should be able to explain the godly meaning of earth and water."[30]

The demon then explained to Ananda that in his past life he had been a dog. "One day I barked when I saw a *paccekabuddha*[31] on his alms rounds. By announcing the *paccekabuddha*'s presence, which had gone unnoticed, my owner was able to give alms to the holy man. Although I'm a Yakkha in this life," the demon explained, "because of that meritorious deed I will have an opportunity to become a follower of the Buddha (literally, to obey the precepts)." But the Yakkha continued to hold Ananda firmly in his grasp because he was unable to solve the demon's puzzle.

The Buddha, seeing by his supernatural power that Ananda had been captured by the Yakkha, arose from his resting place and went to the Ping River, even though he was in great pain. When the Buddha approached, the demon asked him to explain the godly meaning of the elements of earth and water. The Buddha answered him, "Earth means one who is endowed with a sense of shame and fear of wrongdoing." After hearing this explanation the demon released one of Ananda's arms. The Buddha then said that water means one who makes amends for one's life and is suffused with peace. Then the Yakkha released Ananda's other arm. Awestruck [by the Buddha's wisdom] the demon became a lay follower of the Blessed One, exclaiming, "Indeed, you are the Lord Buddha since you know the godly meaning of the elements of earth and water." Ananda then strained some water from the river for the Buddha to drink before they returned to the mango tree.

After the two of them reached the mango tree, the Buddha smiled and laughed softly. "Why are you laughing?" Ananda asked. "I see that in the future the two white pigs under this tree will be reborn as kings in Lan Chang Ayodhaya and the Yakkha will be reborn as the ruler of the city of Chi Mai which later will be called Chiang Mai," the Buddha replied. "The Yakkha will be King Kawila.[32] In this mango grove the three of them will make a reclining Buddha image [today known as Wat Phra Non in the district of Mae Rim near Chiang Mai]. If people care for the image, they will prosper; if not, they will decline. Worshipping this image will be like venerating the Tathagata himself. Those who do so will receive the three kinds of happiness [body, mind, equanimity] and reach Nirvana."

Following this prediction, the Buddha and Ananda continued on their way. When they had walked for some distance the Buddha felt the urge to relieve himself. A Naga king dug a hole and Indra built a shelter over it. The Buddha predicted that in the future this site would be known as Phra Bat Yang Wit. [Today the monastery, The Holy Footprint Bathroom Resting Place, is located in San Pa Tong district near Chiang Mai.][33]

As Ananda and the Buddha journeyed along the Ping River toward the southwest, the Blessed One was overcome with pain. The Tathagata sat down to rest in the shade of an Asoka tree while Ananda spread out the Blessed One's outer robe to dry. A Lawa farmer irrigating his paddy field nearby mistook the Buddha for a Yakkha, threw down his hoe and fled in fear. As he was running away, the Blessed One called out to him, "O lay disciple, come here. Don't be afraid. I'm not a demon; I'm the Lord Buddha." Because of the Buddha's majestic bearing, the Lawa farmer approached him and sat down. As they were sitting under the tree, mucus dripped from the

Buddha's nose but miraculously floated up to the leaves of the Asoka tree giving the leaves a golden hue. Ananda collected the mucus-glazed leaves and made them into a beautiful relic which he gave to the Lawa farmer. Indra, who together with the *arahant* monks and Vissukamma had joined the Buddha and Ananda, made a reliquary tower. Afterwards, the Buddha spoke to them, "This relic will be here as long as you live. In the future it will be known as Chom Thong because the relic was given to the farmer on the leaves of a Thong tree. This relic has the power to determine who is good and who is evil.

Following this prediction, the Buddha departed [walking toward a mountain south of Chiang Mai]. The sun was unbearably hot, greatly increasing the Blessed One's discomfort. Indra and Vissukama brought a sacred umbrella and held it to protect the Buddha from the sun. Hence, this place has been called Mount Doi Kaeng [to protect or shade from the sun] until today.

Realizing that his death was at hand, the Buddha decided to travel to Kusinara. Observing that he was exhausted and hungry, Indra and Vissukamma brought three myrobalan fruits from Tavatimsa Heaven in a golden bowl and offered them to the Blessed One. "*Bhante*," they said, "please eat the myrobalan fruit and you will feel better." At first the Buddha refused [knowing his end was near], but later ate one. Ananda took the seed and planted it about two thousand meters to the west of Mount Doi Kaeng [in Hot district]. "Whoever eats the fruit of this myrobalan tree will be free from disease," Ananda predicted. Afterwards, still in great pain, the Buddha journeyed to Kusinara. He reached the Jetavana forest at sunrise on Tuesday of the month of Visakha, the sixth month of the northern Thai calendar. The Blessed One would die on that day.

At that time the Buddha, by his mental powers, saw a Yakkha who lived on Sacred Water Basin Mountain (Doi Ang Salung) in Hariphunchai.[34] Afterwards, he went to the Doi Ang Salung to practice an ascetic regimen. At that time the Yakkha who lived on the mountain went in search for someone to eat and happened to see the Buddha. "How lucky I am today to have happened upon someone to eat," thought the Yakkkha, and he rushed to attack the Buddha with all of his awesome power.

The Buddha, perceiving the intention of the Yakkha warned him as follows, "O Lord Yakkha, do not eat me. The evil consequences of this deed would be inexhaustible. I'm not an ordinary person. I'm the Fully Enlightened One, the Ruler of the Three Worlds." The demon was so overwhelmed and frightened that he nearly shook to death. Assuming the form of a human being he bowed down before the Buddha and asked the Blessed One's forgiveness. Then, taking leave of the Tathagata he returned to his cave in the mountain and reported his experience to his wife. "Today a miraculous thing happened to me," he said. "I went out to find someone to eat, and met a person with a radiant, golden hue. As I attacked him this resplendent being said, "Do not eat me. You will suffer the consequences of this evil deed forever. I'm not an ordinary being. I'm the Lord of the Three Worlds." When I heard this I was so frightened that I bowed down before him and then returned to the cave."

When the Yakkha's wife heard this story, she realized that the person her husband had encountered was the Fully Enlightened Lord Buddha, so she advised him as follows "O, husband, the man you met was no ordinary person but one of great merit. He is the Lord Buddha. If you had killed and eaten him you would never have escaped the evil consequences of this deed. You must take offerings of flowers to the Blessed One and beg his forgiveness. Following his wife's advice, the demon hurried to get fragrant flowers to offer to the Buddha. Taking an offering of flowers, he approached the Buddha saying, "O Blessed One, you who have transcended suffering, to you I present these offerings and beg your forgiveness for having attacked you. Please teach me your dharma.

At that time the Lord Buddha foresaw that the Yakkha, due to his past merit, would become a famous person in the future. Therefore, he accepted the demon's offering and forgave him. The Blessed One then taught him the three refuges and the five precepts. After hearing the Buddha's teaching, the Yakkha took the refuges and the precepts, promising to refrain from killing, stealing, adultery, lying, and intoxicants, and to serve the Buddha.

An Apocalyptic Vision of the Kala Yuga. The Righteous Ruler

The Blessed One then preached the following *tamnan:*[35] "In the third millennium following my death you will be reborn as a righteous ruler.[36] You will live for two hundred years and you will be a strong supporter of my religion. There will be four other righteous rulers. Of the five, one will be King Asoka who will reign in Pataliputta. Another, a merchant who sells costly *miang*[37] for seventy pieces of silver a packet, will rule in Hongsawadi [Pegu].[38] The third, a person who sells salt for 3,300 *rupees* or seventy-two pieces of silver, will govern in Ava.[39] The fourth, a person who sells a hundred betel leaves for thirty pieces of silver, will rule in Ayodhaya [Lan Chang].[40] The fifth will be a person who sells rice for seventy pieces of silver a measure.[41]

"The five righteous kings will rule for the five thousand years my religion will flourish after my death. The first, Asoka will reign in the first millennium; during the second millennium, Aniruddha the seller of *miang*, will govern Hongsawadi or Pegu; in the third millennium, the seller of rice will rule in Yonok Hariphunchai;[42] during the fourth millennium, the person who sells betel leaves will govern Lan Chang Ayodhaya Dvaravati;[43] in the fifth millennium the person who sells salt will reign in Ava. My religion will flourish for five thousand years. In the third millennium you will be the righteous king who will rule in Chiang Dao.[44] This large mountain is called Doi Aung Salung Chiang Dao. It is very wide and rises to a height of sixteen kilometers. It has an enormous cave with a Buddha image two thousand meters high. A Naga king accompanied by an army of ten thousand protects the image.

"A thousand years after my death the queen of the city of Mueang Phing [Chiang Mai], known as Nagara Siyam in Pali, will convince her husband, Phaya Hua Kian, to steal from ministers and the people, placing the blame on someone else. Furthermore, everyday he will wander about in a drunken stupor. As a result of his immoral behavior, his ministers will replace the king with a lineage who will rule the city through a succession of twenty monarchs. Soon after the twentieth king begins his rule a war will break out in Kosambi.[45] It will spread to Hariphunchai. It will be a dark age and many people will die in war, but in the year *kat rao*[46] a righteous ruler will appear at Chiang Dao who will bring peace. Under him Buddhism will thrive. In the year *poek san*, the Lord Indra will descend from Tavatimsa Heaven. He will sound the bronze drum and blow the conch shell to call together all the people of Jambudipa to give alms to the monks, keep the five precepts, listen to the dharma, and practice loving-kindness.

[Let me further elaborate.] "The evil among the people and the monastic order will lead to war, starvation, disease, pestilence, and death. Rice will be very expensive. People born during that time will not practice charity, loving-kindness, or meditation. [In this evil time] a person of great merit will appear, a rice merchant who will become a righteous ruler. He will go to Din Daeng Mountain in the area of Fang.[47] Indra will take his staff and his horse, Kanthaka,[48] and will follow him to Din Daeng Mountain. He will say to the merchant, 'Please go with me to the junction of three rivers.' There Indra will give him three lumps of sticky rice and say, 'Look after my horse. If you get hungry eat the rice. If the horse begins to quiver, mount and it will quiet down.' Indra will then depart.

"The merchant, being overcome with hunger, will eat the three lumps of rice, and the horse will quiver. He will then mount the horse and it will fly up into the air. The ten thousand worlds will resound with the glad cries of the four world guardians, the celestial beings, the demons, and the celestial musicians. The people in Jambudipa, hearing the loud commotion, will be startled and afraid. Then Indra, the world guardians, the deities, the demons, the celestial musicians, the Yakkha and Naga will accompany the righteous ruler to Tavatimsa Heaven where he will be consecrated before descending to Hariphunchai to be consecrated again at Doi Ang Salung Chiang Dao.[49] Indra and the gods will perform the royal consecration at the three palaces situated around Doi Aung Salung Chiang Dao, each rising to a height of seventy-four meters, one made of diamonds, another of silver, and a third of gold. Around the palaces on each side will be a moat through which flows water from ponds at each of the four corners."

The gods and all of those gathered there arranged the royal consecration for the rice merchant who was the son of the potter. He was a righteous ruler and a person of great merit. On this occasion one thousand six hundred divine Kanlapaphruek trees spontaneously arose from the ground around Chiang Dao.[50] The news of this miraculous event spread throughout Jambudipa. Everyone came. They piled up their old clothing making a mound seven cubits high. A strong wind blew seven times scattering the clothing everywhere. The Kanlapaphruek trees then showered down new clothes and adornments for those who were meritorious.

All the people of Kosambi paid respects to the king and served him. The mendicants and priests who did not follow the monastic rules (*vinaya*) of the Buddha were made to disrobe. The monks who followed the precepts and the *vinaya* continued to teach the Buddha's religion. The serenity of Jambudipa at that time was like the shade of a Nigroda tree. The righteous king ruled for two hundred years due to his merit. From the year *ruang kai*, however, many troubles arose and the people suffered greatly.

The Story of the Buddha's Journey Resumes

[At that time] the people asked the Buddha for his footprint. Observing that there was no suitable place for a footprint he went to the east where he sat down on a rock and predicted that a great city would appear there and where he left his footprint his religion would prosper. The Buddha then put his footprint on the rock where he had been resting, and afterwards sat down under a *bunnak* tree.[51] The tree had been planted by an old man who made a living by selling the tree's flowers. While the Buddha was sitting there, the old man and his wife went up to the *bunnak* tree and presented him with an offering of flowers from the tree. The Lord Buddha then predicted that a large monastery would be built there which would be called the Puppharam Monastery.[52]

After that the *arahant* monks and King Asoka, the righteous ruler, spoke respectfully to the Lord Buddha, "O Blessed One, in the future your religion will prosper here. Therefore, we request that a relic be enshrined in this place." Honoring this request, the Lord Buddha took a hair relic, gave it to King Asoka, and said, "One hair relic is insufficient. There should be reliquaries in eight locations." The Tathagata then placed the strand of hair in his right hand and made the following resolve (*adhitthan*),[53] "This place will become an important reliquary. May this strand of hair multiply eightfold." The single strand of hair then multiplied into eight identical strands of equal length. The Lord Indra and King Asoka then took one of the hairs and enshrined it at the place where the Lord Buddha had been sitting. This was called Wat Puppharam Suan Dok.

The Lord Buddha continued on his journey toward the northeast until he came to a clump of bamboo. He predicted that a monastery would be established there called Veluvanarama [the Bamboo

Stalactite formation in Chiang Dao cave

Monastery].[54] The *arahant* monks and King Asoka enshrined a second hair relic there. Walking easterly toward Wat Puppharam, the Buddha encountered two roughly attired Burmese ascetics. Seeing the Buddha, they asked to be ordained by the Tathagata which he did with the formula, "Come Monks." The Lord Buddha then predicted that in the future a large city would be established at that place called Anagatanagara or Chi Mai, known as Chiang Mai today.[55]

Journeying southward, the Buddha encountered two Lawa shooting wild buffalo. Upon seeing the Lord Buddha they offered him rice and buffalo meat. The Buddha responded by predicting that in the future a large monastery would be established there called Asokarama since at that spot two Tamila [Lawa] had offered him dried buffalo meat. Subsequently, the monks and King Asoka asked the Buddha for a hair relic which they enshrined at the place later called Asokarama.

Leaving there, the Buddha continued further south until he sat down [to rest]. [Seeing the Buddha], two Lawa at that place presented the Blessed One with two mangoes, ripe plums, ripe jackfruit, and rice. They also offered him saffron rice, fragrant oil, and water to wash his face. After the Buddha [had eaten] and washed, he preached to the Lawa for three days and nights. He predicted that in the future a large monastery named Kiccarama would be built there. King Asoka enshrined a hair relic at that spot.

Subsequently, the Buddha went toward the northeast where he met seven Burmese monks. They requested a hair relic from the Buddha and enshrined it at a place called Sangharama from that time until today. Walking further north the Buddha encountered a Lawa[56] who built a hut for the Buddha and invited him to stay. With loving-kindness he accepted the Lawa's offer for one night, predicting that in the future a large monastery named Indarama would be built on the site of the hut. King Asoka took a hair relic and enshrined it at that place. The Lawa then invited the Lord Buddha to visit his home village. Filled with faith, the villagers erected flags and banners in honor of the Buddha.[57]

There was a Burmese ascetic who had reached the age of one hundred and two. Upon seeing the Buddha he was filled with faith and exclaimed, "My one hundred and two years were wasted until I met the Lord Buddha. Now that I have seen you I am truly blessed." He then took one of his robes, dipped it in oil, and ignited it [as a lamp] in honor of the Buddha. The Lord Buddha acknowledged this offering by saying, "Out of compassion the Tathagata will leave a hair relic here."

The Lord Buddha then crossed the Ping River to the north. Spying a stone shaped like a tortoise, he sat down [to rest]. A Naga king who lived there paid respects to the Buddha and together with the monks and King Asoka asked the Blessed One for a relic so that his religion might prosper in that place. The Lord Buddha replied, "Because there is no cave here, it is an unsuitable location to enshrine a relic." Thereupon, the monks, Lord Indra, and King Asoka asked, "If this place is inappropriate for a relic, will you please leave a footprint instead?" The Blessed One consented, making a footprint about four cubits deep and four cubits wide so that both human beings and deities could honor him there.

Continuing to the north along the Ping River for about eight kilometers, he encountered a ferocious Naga. The evil Naga wanted to eat the Lord Buddha, but by his miraculous power the Blessed One froze him in his tracks. Realizing that the Buddha's power exceeded his own, the Naga said, "If you are enlightened release me from the trance under which I have been placed." After the Lord Buddha had done so, the demon prepared a stone seat for him four cubits wide and then offered the Blessed One food. Since the Buddha had no water to drink, the Naga presented some to him in a golden bowl. After the Lord Buddha had eaten, the Naga became a follower of the Buddha [literally, requested the five precepts]. The Naga was so overjoyed that he removed both of his eyes and presented them to the Tathagata as a gift, and out of gratitude spread his hood over the Blessed One as protection and asked the Lord Buddha to leave a footprint. Looking toward the east, the Buddha made a footprint in the stone with the following prediction, "Because the Naga king gave his eyes to me as offering, a great city will be built at this place." After paying respects to the Lord Buddha, the Naga returned to his home. His eyes were restored, brighter and more luminous than before.

As the Lord Buddha continued in an easterly direction he reflected, "I am old and with only a short time remaining before I die, I have not yet enshrined a relic here." Sadness arose in the Tathagata at the realization that in the future only a few relics would be found there. Continuing further to the east for a distance of four kilometers, he came to the house of a Lawa merchant who made and sold clay pots. The merchant asked the Lord Buddha where he was going. The Buddha replied, "The Tathagata is going to this city for the welfare of many." The wealthy merchant then said, "You are the Enlightened One. Please remain here seven days," and he prepared a dwelling place for the Blessed One. [The next morning] the villagers presented food to the Blessed One as he went on his morning alms rounds. After he had eaten he made the following prediction, "In the future a large city name Bhuñjanagara [Hariphunchai] will be built here," [Following this prediction] the *arahant* monks and King Asoka requested a hair relic from the Lord Buddha so his religion would prosper. Headed by the wealthy merchant, the Lawa, King

Asoka, and the monks enshrined the relic in a deep hole. They put the relic in a bamboo container that, in turn, was put in a lacquer box eight cubits high. Placing the relic in the hole along with many costly objects, they built a golden *chedi* over it protected by a revolving wheel (*yanta-cakka*) made by Indra.[58] Afterwards the Blessed One told the monks and King Asoka that a bone relic from the right side of his head would be enshrined there after his death.

The Lord Buddha walked to the north for about twenty kilometers until he met a Lawa and a Burmese who gave the Buddha a packet of betel nut as an offering.[59] About noon the Lord Buddha spoke to the monks and King Asoka, "In the future this place where the Burmese gave the Tathagata a packet of betel will be known as Thi Cha or Kum Kam.[60] Then the *arahant* monks and King Asoka, the righteous ruler, asked the Buddha to offer a relic so his religion would prosper in that place. The Lord Buddha gave a hair relic to the monks, King Asoka, the Lawa, and a Burmese. They placed a relic in a bamboo container that they put in a lacquer box seven cubits high and then buried it in a hole one hundred eleven cubits deep. The Burmese placed many valuable objects in the hole. Indra protected the relic with a revolving wheel and made a covering two cubits high. The Lord Buddha then made the following prediction, "After the Tathagata has passed away his right liver will be enshrined here as a relic."

The *arahant* monks, King Asoka, a Naga king, and Ananda all spent the night there while the Buddha slept under a tamarind tree at Doi Mon Noi located to the south. The tree was twenty meters in girth and six cubits high. The tree deities were overjoyed and honored the Buddha with a shower of diamonds and gold. In the morning the gold and diamonds had reached all the way to the mountain and for this reason the mountain is called Doi Khao Kham Luang.[61]

A Golden Deer and a White Rabbit Discuss the Future.
The Apocalyptic Vision Continues

At that time a deity in the form of a golden deer came to Chiang Dao from the north. Another became a white rabbit and came to Chiang Dao from the south. The deer asked the rabbit, "O friend, from where do you come?" The rabbit replied, "I come from the south." The golden deer then said, "O friend, you are known as a very wise person. I would like to ask you a question. If you know the answer please tell me. Will your country be peaceful and happy?" The rabbit answered, "No, my country will be very troubled. Evil people will undermine the social order and immoral monks will contaminate the *sangha* just as dirty water pollutes a clean pond. There will be no peace or order.[62] Horses will graze with water buffalo; they will be tethered rather than allowed to roam freely. Men will behave in a strange manner: they will cover their head and eyes, walk around carrying spears, and wear ear-rings like women. Merchants will act like officials; monks like lay persons. Sages will be without virtue; rulers will spend time fretting over their wardrobe rather than administering the kingdom. People will fashion flags out of handkerchiefs; large-headed ghosts will circle in the air; and rain will fall out of season. No one will follow the dharma: monks and laity will regard sermons as evil rather than good; they will not observe the precepts, nor will they practice loving-kindness or meditate. They will perform evil deeds and be indifferent to the consequences; even their good acts will produce no merit. People will not respect wise sages or monks; immoral folk will attack their teachers and honor monks who fail to keep the discipline. Monks will dress and behave like lay persons; teachers will consider stupid, contemptuous things as good; scholars and learned men will live by customs contrary to the teaching of the Buddha; the ruler, his ministers, and everyone else will not follow the way of right conduct. They will reject the Triple Gem, the lineage of the king and respected elders, and will substitute new customs in their place.

"It will be a time dominated by evildoers, war, and suffering. Ten-year-old girls will engage in sexual intercourse; parents will force their female children to marry; husbands and wives will commit adultery, and families will disintegrate. At the beginning of the third millennium after the founding of the Buddha's religion, the monastic order will decline; people will not respect those with knowledge; they will sell images and amulets of the Buddha and of the king; both monks and laity, old and young, scholars and ordinary folk will not know the difference between right and wrong, good and evil. They will be illiterate and without skills; discipline and tradition will disappear. Lay people will not respect monks who observe the *vinaya*, and both laity and monks will follow their own selfish interests, doing whatever they please.

"Pretending to be wise, philosophers will teach only falsehoods and monks will not study the dharma. Undisciplined laymen interested only in eating and sleeping will ordain as monks; they will be governed by greed and craving; they will not seek the way to heaven or nirvana but will perform only those things that lead to continuous rebirth. Gold and silver will be less valuable than cowrie shells and cheaper than rice. The wealthy will make pots and pans out of gold and silver and throw away valuable objects unaware of their true worth. Immoral people will reject the traditions and customs of the elders; they will quarrel and insult one another.

"There will be destruction and death. The lineage of the righteous ruler will be destroyed. Others who come to rule will impose heavy taxes. No one capable of ruling the country will come to the fore. It will be a time of oppression and persecution beyond human endurance. [Everything will be turned upside down.] Low classes will usurp power from the high classes; the ruling nobles will become slaves; children will treat adults disrespectfully and adults will neglect their children. Hatred will reign.

"The air will resound with loud thunder like the braying of a donkey or the sound of cannon; crows will fly up into air only to fall back down again to the earth, and vultures will circle the sky. The sky will be covered with clouds but no rain will fall; trees will bloom out of season; rice will not ripen in the fields; rice paddies and water wells will dry up. Crops will be stunted and the rice fields will lie fallow; the starving people will desert their villages. Lightning, looking like long banners will strike the earth time and again; rainbows will bend down out of the sky to steal water from the wells of villages and towns.

"It will be a time devoid of merit. The guardian spirit of the monastery will become the village teacher, and the people will worship him. The people will drink alcohol and slaughter animals at temple ceremonies. Monks will dress like commoners, wear hats, carry swords, drink liquor, and be controlled by their cravings; they will sing rather than chant; they will disrobe and go to war. Sages will propagate false views; merchants will steal; teachers will be drunkards; the learned will not respect the dharma; and not one can be found who observes the precepts.

"The powerful will unjustly persecute the weak. Those who lack merit will become rulers. Their rule will be so oppressive that people will be forced to flee, but nowhere will they be able to find a justly governed country. They will oppress both commoners and slaves, and commoners will be forced to buy their freedom. Large cities will become towns which, in turn, will be reduced to small villages; large houses will become small; and, small houses will become huts. Cities will be destroyed, and people will flee to the forest. Enemies will lurk everywhere and the people will starve. O friend, this calamity will effect everyone. Everyone in Jambudipa will starve and suffer."

After the rabbit had made this prediction, the golden deer asked, "O friend, when will this story of devastation be over?" The rabbit replied, "My friend, I am not yet finished. From the year *kap chai* until the year *rawai chai* calamities will continue. There will be seven great earthquakes. All of the states in Jambudipa will engage in brutal, destructive wars. Blood will flood the earth." The deer again asked, "O friend, is the story over yet?" His friend replied, "No, my friend, not yet. From the year *rawai chai* until the year *kot yi* one kingdom will be without royal elephants; in another women will find no husbands; and in still another there will be an overabundance of food but none who can purchase it.

"Finally, in the year *kat rao* in the seventh month on the seventh day, a righteous ruler will appear on the banks of the Huai Kai [Chiang Mai] river which flows from Lake Phaya Nang Kachok. At his birth everyone—nobility, commoners, priests, and ascetics—will honor him. He will be endowed with wisdom and teach the citizens the way of goodness. Indra, Brahma, the gods, and celestial beings will perform the royal consecration for the righteous king who will rule in Chiang Dao."

At that time, it was Vissukamma who appeared as a golden deer and conversed with the white rabbit. The Buddha made this prediction in his sermon to the Lord of the Yakkhas. This is the *tamnan* of the relic and footprint.

Doi Ang Salung Chiang Dao

Now we will continue the *tamnan*. After the Buddha passed away at Kusinara, five hundred of his disciples took the Buddha's relics and those of five hundred *arahant* monks to Doi Ang Salung in the kingdom of Chiang Dao. The Lord Indra, Brahma, the gods, celestial beings, and King Ananda Rajapingmuang, the ruler of Chiang Dao, built a large golden *chedi* to a height of six hundred meters for the Buddha relics. A hermit by the name of Brahma dwelt on the mountain forty-eight meters high. Together with the gods Indra, Brahma, the guardians of the earth, and a Naga king by the name of Virubakkha they made a golden standing image of the Buddha fourteen meters high for both divine and human beings to venerate. This precious image was erected in the cave of Chiang Dao. Even those who see it from a distance and venerate the image make merit. Such an act guarantees them a long and successful life. The image is located in a beautiful area six hundred meters from the entrance to the cave. The Anomanadi River flows into the cave from under the base of the image. The image is filled with gold, silver, and adorned with seven precious gems. It is placed on a pedestal twenty-four meters high. Thirty steps ascend to the top of the pedestal.

The ruler of the Yakkhas, Chao Luang Kham Daeng, with ten thousand attendants, guard the cave. In the cave are sacred emblems, a precious golden Bodhi tree, a golden Buddha image, and a golden *chedi*. Chao Luang Kham Daeng and his ten thousand attendants watch over these precious objects which are encircled by a fence. They also guard the space of six hundred meters from the entrance to this place. From the entrance, paths continue in several directions. One goes to the place of a meditating hermit; a second to [the image of] Chao Luang Kham Daeng; a third to a golden Bodhi tree; a fourth to a Naga; a fifth to the Erawan elephant and a Yakkha; a sixth goes to a golden *chedi;* a seventh to a golden Buddha image on a base covered with precious gems. These paths are covered with gold and silver sand. One hundred eighty meters beyond these paths one comes to a river with huts for six monks. On the bank of the river one will see a set of sacred clothes. If you put them on, gardens and a village will appear before you.

From there are seven more golden paths. One goes to the top of the mountain and then descends on the backside. Another goes beside the village about one and a half kilometers to a large lake one hundred eighty meters wide. At the northern border there is an opening about the size of the mouth of a large water jar. One should make an offering of sweet and bitter curries, coconut, nine candles, nine flower bouquets to the deities of the nine directions.

Afterwards, pass through the opening for about two to four meters. There you will see a prosperous Naga city. If a monk enters he must wear his outer robe. Anyone who enters—monk, lay person, *brahman* ascetic—should fast beforehand. If they eat anything they will not be able to return, but if they do so quickly, then they can return and upon reaching home they should fast for seven days.

To see the garden, walk about one hundred forty meters from the entrance. After walking one and a half kilometers further, you will see a bronze image of the Buddha made by Chao Luang Kham Daeng. There you should make offerings of sweet and sour curries, one hundred candles, seven red and seven white cloth banners. Look behind the Buddha image and you will see a hermit meditating there. Offer seven kinds of flowers to him. Beyond that is Chao Luang Kham Daeng's golden pavilion. There offer four candles, four bouquets of flowers, two cups of milk, and nine containers of sugar. Afterwards go about eight hundred meters where one comes to a river chest deep. The Erawan elephant is there. Offer nine bunches of grass and eleven stalks of sugar cane. Walk about a kilometer and a half to a wall about twelve meters high and you will see a Buddha image sixteen meters tall. Another stream flows from the base of this image. It is covered with seven precious gems. Stairs of gold and silver ascend from the base of the pedestal to the top.[63]

Ten thousand Yakkhas guard Doi Ang Salung. Whoever enters the cave—monk, laity, *brahman* ascetic—should first bathe and take the five or eight precepts, and offer flowers, puffed rice, three hundred gold and three hundred silver candles, four flowering plants, eight flags each in black, red, yellow, and white, and one thousand small clay lamps. By making these offerings, one will be greatly rewarded by the guardian Yakkhas and will be able to leave the cave. Moreover, if one enters the cave to make offerings to the Buddha and the relic, to keep the precepts, and to practice meditation, one will enjoy good fortune.

Doi Ang Salung Chiang Dao is a place where Buddha image, Buddha relic, and relics of all the previous Buddhas, *arahant* monks, and hermits are kept. The wise will care for the image and relics. Everyone who knows this *tamnan* and pays respects to the Buddha image, and the relics of the Buddhas and the *arahant*s at Doi Ang Salung, whether they come from far or near will make merit beyond calculation.

This short history of Doi Ang Salung is now complete. I finished copying it on Thursday, June 5, at 3:00 P.M. in the year *kap san*, C.S. 1306 [1944 C.E.]. Copied by Phra Tha Bhikkhu for the success of the religion at Wat Nong Chang, the village of Ban Paen in the district of Lamphun. By this act may I reach Nirvana. If you want to know more you should read the *Tamnan Buddha Nimitta*.

THE LEGEND OF CHAO LUANG KHAM DAENG, LORD BURNISHED GOLD[64]

Chao Luang Kham Daeng was the son of the king of Mueang Champa [Phayao] about one hundred fifty kilometers northeast of Doi Luang Chiang Dao. The king had one son and six older daughters. The six daughters were all married. Only the son remained at home. Within the borders of the kingdom there were many towns such as Mueang Phing [Chiang Mai], Chaiyapakan [Fang], and Angwa [Ava]. The town of Angwa was about two hundred kilometers southwest of Doi Luang Chiang Dao. The thirty-year-old ruler of Angwa was powerful and aggressively hostile. He decided to launch an attack on Champa because at fifty-two the king of Champa was old and vulnerable. He sent an emissary to the king warning him that if he did not surrender, the Angwa army would attack within seven days.[65]

Upon receiving the warning from the emissary, the king of Champa pondered where he might get help and consulted his generals and ministers. The king knew full well that he could not defeat the forces of Angwa in battle. They were youthful, stalwart, and fearless after being victorious against many other city-states without suffering a single defeat. The king's officials advised him to summon his six sons-in-law to lead Champa's armies, however, they were afraid to offer their services which made Champa's leaders furious. At last, the king's generals said, "Hope is not lost. There is still your young son, Chao Luang Kham Daeng." A royal page invited the prince to the meeting of the king and Champa's leaders where he readily agreed to lead the army. He asked for ten thousand mounted troops armed with lances and swords so that they could quickly strike at the enemy from an ambush. At Chao Luang Kham Daeng's command all of the weapons, provisions, and carriages were readied. At that time the prince was only sixteen years old but he

Shrine to Chao Luang Kham Daeng near the entrance to Doi Chiang Dao cave

was physically strong, had studied the arts and sciences, and was very wise.

At an auspicious time the prince and his troops marched toward the southwest for seven days but they caught no sight of the enemy. Chao Luang Kham Daeng then ordered his troops to bivouac at a place with an abundant water supply where today there is a bend in the Ping River. They crossed to the other shore and camped on a hillock from which they could quickly attack the enemy. After finishing the encampment the weary prince quickly fell asleep.

Early the next morning a forest rooster was heard and as the sun rose crows flew out from the thick of the forest while elephants gamboled. Some of the soldiers readied their weapons while others stacked provisions. After Chao Luang Kham Daeng awoke he went for a walk in the forest. Admiring the beauty of his natural surroundings he felt refreshed. Suddenly he spied a golden deer happily nibbling grass around a large tree. The prince called the soldiers to come and confirm what he saw. "Yes," they exclaimed, "it's a golden deer." Chao Luang Kham Daeng ordered the soldiers to make a circle around the golden deer. "If the deer comes toward any of you," he said, "grab it and prevent it from escaping." When the soldiers made a circle around the golden deer, it was startled and began running back and forth, sometimes stopping and at other times going around in circles.[66]

The prince was entranced by the deer's beauty. Seeing that Chao Luang Kham Daeng was in a trance-like state, she ran towards him and jumped through the circle where the prince stood. The prince rode after her on horseback until he came to an unfamiliar forest called Pa Phuan (Invisible Forest). Chao Luang Kham Daeng had his soldiers surround the forest in an even smaller circle. The golden deer saw no way to escape [if she stayed where she was] so she emerged from her hiding place in the dense woods and continued her flight. Chao Luang Kham Daeng followed her until the golden deer began to tire. The prince then ordered his soldiers to advance quickly [and for that reason] this place is called Advance Village. As the deer continued to flee she was intercepted by the soldiers, [and for this reason] this place is called Intercept Village (Ban Mae Dae). Then the golden deer ran into Intercept Forest with Chao Luang Kham Daeng and his soldiers in hot pursuit. Seeing them closing in, she cast off her deer body so that when the prince and the soldiers arrived they would see only a deer corpse, [and for this reason] the place is called Corpse Village. Although they searched high and low, the soldiers found no evidence of the golden deer. Chao Luang Kham Daeng saw only a beautiful, nude maiden with bright white skin. The prince urged his horse to follow after her. Coming to a brook, the woman fell exhausted into the water. Chao Luang Kham Daeng, thinking that the large number of male soldiers might frighten her, held up his hand for them to halt. Stepping out of the water the maiden continued to run until she came to another brook where she paused to look back. The prince signaled for the soldiers to bow down, [and so] this brook is called Prostrate Creek. As the young woman continued her flight, the sun grew quite hot for it was midday so when she reached another brook she knelt down and with cupped hands quenched her thirst, [and so] this brook is called Quenched Thirst Creek. Reaching a hillock, the beautiful girl hid in a stone cave with the prince and his soldiers still in pursuit. When she was seen by them she ran to the top of the hill around which the soldiers began to dig a moat three levels deep to prevent her escape. After they had finished the second level the young woman realized that she would not be able to escape if they finished the third so she again fled from her hiding place. The prince, spying her, followed on his horse. The maiden ran quickly to a high mountain with Chao Luang Kham Daeng following behind. This mountain is called Woman Mountain (Doi Nang) and is north of Doi Chiang Dao. Here she stopped and asked the prince, "Why are you chasing me?" Chao Luang Kham Daeng answered that she was the most incomparably beautiful woman in the world. The young woman responded, "Are you like every other man in the world, only interested in sex?" "Oh, no, my fair lady, your incomparable beauty compels me to speak only the truth."

"Men don't remain truthful to women for a very long time," she said. "When they've got what they want, all the sweetness disappears; they lose interest and leave."

"That's not true [for me]," the prince replied. "Your beauty is unlike any other in the world. Therefore, I wanted only to speak truthfully from my heart." To this the woman said, "A man's commitment to a woman soon fades. When he gets what he wants all the sweetness evaporates and he loses interest."

"It's because you possess such goodness that I wanted to meet you," continued Chao Luang Kham Daeng. "I won't be so easily dissuaded." To this the young woman responded, "What's the hurry? I don't even know you. How can I love you?"

"I'm Chao Luang Kham Daeng, the son of the king of Champa. I was on my way to confront an enemy on behalf of my father. I would die willingly with the satisfaction of knowing that you let me serve you."

"As for me," the woman replied, "I live at home with my aged mother. Everyday I go out looking for food for I am still under my mother's care. If you want [to marry] me, you must request permission from my mother." Chao Luang Kham Daeng then followed the woman into a large cave [in Doi Chiang Dao] but before leaving he promised his soldiers, "I'll return in seven days if not earlier."

The soldiers were very worried about the prince but, not knowing what else to do, they returned to their camp on the hill to wait. That evening they staged entertainment to celebrate the marriage of Chao Luang Kham Daeng even though it was unofficial. The village at this place is called the Entertainment Field. After seven days had elapsed and Chao Luang Kham Daeng still had not appeared, the soldiers searched everywhere but as no sign of the prince was to be found they broke camp and returned to Champa. Doubting that the woman [with whom Chao Luang Kham Daeng went into the cave] was Chamathewi[67] the king said, "The real Chamathewi isn't very beautiful so I'm sure the woman was the demon In Lao. She was out looking for a human being to eat just at the time my son happened along so he became a meal for her. When In Lao is out and about looking for food it is a bad time to go into battle."

In his great sorrow [over his son's death], the king of Champa had his army build a shrine to Chao Luang Kham Daeng in front of the cave.[68] He then sponsored a ceremony to call on all of the powerful spirits to protect the people. To this very day a ceremony is held on the fifteenth day of the waxing moon during the month of April [?] in which the spirit of Chao Luang Kham Daeng is invoked and the precepts are observed as a memorial to the time when the Yakkha, In Lao, devoured the prince in the cave. In Lao's entourage swore allegiance to Chao Luang Kham Daeng [whose spirit guards the cave]. He resides in the cave attended by the ascetic, Brahma, where he continues to be nurtured in the dharma.

Chao Luang Kham Daeng rules over the spirits and lords of the forest and the mountains in northern Thailand all the way to the Burma border. Those who are under the suzerainty of Chao Luang Kham Daeng come together annually at Doi Ang Salung. At the celebration a feast of live animals is arranged by the spirits themselves.[69]

DOI SUTHEP:
WASUTHEP MOUNTAIN AND
THE LEGEND OF DOI KHAM

INTRODUCTION

Doi Suthep and its environs were first inhabited by the Lawa, a Mon-Khmer group who lived in the area prior to the major Tai migrations into northern Thailand in the thirteenth century. From the time King Mangrai established Chiang Mai as his capital in 1292 C.E., the city has been the dominant power in northern Thailand. Physically the mountain orients the valley's inhabitants; ecologically its watershed sustains an ever-growing population; and its forest cover is home to an impressive diversity of flora and fauna that includes over 253 species of orchids, 320 bird and 50 mammal species, and more than 500 species of butterflies. Species of previously unknown plants and animals continue to be discovered on Doi Suthep. The mountain region has a rich mythological past and claims one of the most revered Buddhist sanctuaries in mainland Southeast Asia near its summit. A summer palace was built for the country's reigning monarch on Doi Pui, a neighboring peak, and both the temple-monastery, Wat Phra That Doi Suthep, and the royal palace are within the Doi Suthep–Pui National Park that extends over 162 square kilometers.

In the manner of classical Theravada Buddhist chronicles, the *Tamnan Phra That Suthep* places the Buddha's visit to northern Thailand within the context of a universal Buddhist history by beginning with the story of the Blessed One's attainment of enlightenment. Unlike the *Tamnan Ang Salung*, which focuses on the Buddha's mythic, sacralizing travels throughout Lan Na, the chronicle of Suthep Mountain pays scant attention to the Buddha's visit throughout northern Thailand. It only briefly mentions the

Blessed One's encounter with Ya Sae and her son, Wasuthep, and makes no mention of Pu Sae. Instead, the text tells the story of the holy monk Mahasumana Thera and the relic that he brings to Chiang Mai from Sukhothai which is subsequently enshrined at Wat Suan Dok and on Doi Suthep during the reign of King Kue Na (r. 1355–1385). Thus, while the story told in the chronicle certainly contains legendary elements and cannot be regarded as a strictly historical account, nevertheless it has the flavor of history. The historicity of the account is enhanced by a concluding section on the lineage of Chiang Mai kings and their patronage of Wat Phra That Doi Suthep. Consequently, in contrast to the *Tamnan Ang Salung*, the Doi Suthep chronicle not only appears more historical, it includes an account of royal patronage from the founding of the *wat* in 1371 C.E. to the middle of the sixteenth century. The free translation that follows is based on a microfilm copy in the Social Research Institute, Chiang Mai University, of a palm-leaf manuscript in Lan Na script located at Wat Ubosot in the Saraphi district of Chiang Mai. It was transcribed in C.S. 1186 (1824 C.E.).

A published edition of the chronicle (*Tamnan Phra That Doi Suthep*) appeared in 1947 as a cremation volume in honor of the prince of Chiang Mai, Phontri Kaeonawarat. The published version closely follows the copy used for this translation, although discrepancies between the two indicate it was not based on the same manuscript. In a few instances we followed the rendering in the published text.

Because the legends surrounding Doi Suthep and Doi Kham are interconnected, a translation of a section of the Doi Kham chronicle with an account of Pu Sae, Ya Sae, Wasuthep, and Chamathewi is appended. In the absence of a palm-leaf copy of the Doi Kham chronicle, a recently published account written by the current abbot of Wat Phra That Doi Kham, Phra Khru Paladphin, has been utilized.[1]

The abbot has revitalized the monastery with the help of lay supporters from Chiang Mai and Bangkok. New structures have been built, and old ones restored. In addition, the visitor can find statues of personages who appear in the mythic and legendary history of the mountain and *wat*, namely, Queen Chama, Wasuthep, Wilangkha, Pu Sae, and Ya Sae.

TAMNAN PHRA THAT SUTHEP[2]

The Buddha

Having paid homage to the Buddha, the refuge of the world, the nine supermundane teachings,[3] as well as the teaching in the scriptures, the order of perfected monks, and the historical *sangha*, I shall now relate the legend (*tamnan*, *nithan*) of the relic on Mount Suthep. It took the Lord Buddha over twenty incalculable ages plus one hundred thousand great time periods to reach enlightenment. First, he resolved to reach Buddhahood. For seven incalculable ages he told no one, but during the next eight incalculable ages he announced his intention to achieve enlightenment. After the Buddha Dipankara's prediction, for an additional four incalculable ages plus one hundred thousand great time periods he continued striving to reach enlightenment.[4] He practiced the ten perfections, the ten superior perfections, and the ten supreme perfections,[5] for example, the perfection of charity, and the five great sacrifices—worldly goods, children, wife, body, and finally life. He also achieved the three conducts: conduct for the well-being of the world, conduct for the benefit of relatives, and the beneficial conduct befitting a Buddha. Afterwards he became the Buddha superior to all the Brahmas, deities, human beings, celestial musicians, Garudas, Nagas, Yakkhas, Asuras, and animals.[6] He achieved Buddhahood under the Bodhi tree on the full moon day of the month of Visakha. He then preached his first sermon known as Turning the Wheel of the Dharma at the Deer Park in Varanasi on the full moon day of the tenth lunar month (eighth month in central Thailand).

The Buddha Visits Northern Thailand

Once upon a time the Buddha traveled from place to place preaching to the people. After arriving [in northern Thailand] he stopped at the summit of Sugar Cane Mountain and then descended to collect alms food. After receiving food from Ya Sae and her child [Wasuthep] the Buddha returned to the mountain to eat.[7] Ya Sae and her child were pleased to give alms to the Buddha and went to pay respects to him at the mountain's summit. Ya Sae's son was ordained in the order of monks where he was taught meditation following the instructions of the Buddha, and achieved the six higher knowledges.[8] Later, when he found it difficult to observe the rules of the monastic order he became an ascetic known as Suthep. It is said that when the Buddha was on the mountain with his retinue of five hundred *arahant* monks led by Sariputta, he took a hair from his head with his right hand and gave it to Ya Sae and her son. They were overjoyed at receiving the hair relic and asked, "Where shall we enshrine this relic?" The Buddha replied, "The two of you, mother and son, should enshrine the relic here for this is an auspicious mountain."

(After the Buddha passed away, one of his disciples, named Sumana Bhikkhu, and a king would take the relic and enshrine it on this mountain.) Ya Sae and her child gave the hair relic to the god Indra. Taking it from Ya Sae, Indra made a crypt on the summit of the mountain eighteen cubits (*sok*) deep.[9] Indra made a golden tortoise four cubits long and three cubits wide. Then he made three caskets, one of crystal, a second of gold, and a third of silver. Inside [the smallest] he put the hair relic of the Buddha. [He then put the casket] on top of a tortoise [at the bottom of the crypt]. Under the four feet [of the tortoise] were placed a ruby, bloodstone, emerald, and a cat's eye. Afterwards he placed offerings in the crypt in order to worship the relic of the Buddha. Ya Sae and her son also made many

Wasuthep, Wat Phra That Doi Kham

offerings to put in the crypt in honor of the Buddha. Then Indra stationed four demigods headed by Vatta and Bhatta. Each of them had five hundred followers, and were assigned to protect the relic enshrined in Doi Suthep from that time to the present. The story of the enshrinement of the hair relic on Doi Suthep is now finished.

Sumana and the Discovery of the Relic

I shall now relate how the great relic arrived and came to be enshrined on the mountain of Wasuthep [Doi Suthep]. One thousand eight hundred and seventy-five years after the Buddha's death, c.s. 693 (1331 C.E.), a Mahathera named Matima brought Buddhism from Sri Lanka and established it in the Mon city of Pan [Martaban] where it flourished. The king, his ministers, and citizens were so pleased with Matima's virtuous conduct that he was consecrated as Mahaswami and named, Udumbarapuppha Mahaswami. His reputation for virtue and knowledge spread in all directions among towns large and small.

At that time in Sukhothai there were two monks, one named Anomadassi and the other Sumana. They went to study at various monasteries in Ayutthaya. After finishing their studies, they returned to Sukhothai where they joined the monastery of the Sangharaja, named Pubbhatra. From a group of merchants, the two monks heard about the great virtue of the Udumbarapuppha Mahaswami of Martaban and so they traveled there to request ordination into the community of the Mahaswami. Having studied there for a period of five years, they asked to return to Sukhothai. After they had been ordained for [a total of] ten years, they took eight [young men] to be ordained into the sect of Udumbarapuppha Mahaswami at Martaban. The Mahaswami appointed them as preceptors saying, "Buddhism in this Mon city is still relatively new, but [from here] it will be propagated in Thailand where it will flourish for five thousand years. Take the Buddha's religion to Sukhothai." He then sent the ten monks led by Sumana and Anomadassi back to Thailand.

Udumbarapuppha Mahaswami had intended to put Anomadassi's alms bowl over his shoulder [as a sign of precedence] but did so instead with Sumana Thera's alms bowl before sending the two monks to Thailand to establish the Buddha's religion. Anomadassi went to Satchanalai and Sumana to Sukhothai where each carried out the full range of monastic activities including ordination, and establishing the boundaries of ordination halls. Here ends the second chapter that relates the coming of Buddhism [to Thailand].

One night when Sumana Thera was sleeping in the early morning before sunrise, a god appeared to him saying, "Venerable Sir, please listen. King Asoka enshrined a relic of our Lord Buddha in a *chedi* on a mountain at the city of Bangcha but it collapsed. All that remains is a needle flower bush (*dok khem*) that looks like a round stool placed over the relic. This Buddha relic is to be enshrined in the city of Chiang Mai to be worshipped by human beings and gods and flourish for a long time. You should remove the relic, honor it with offerings, and take it to Chiang Mai."

Having been addressed in this manner, Mahasumana Thera immediately awoke, overjoyed at his dream. The following day he informed King Siridhamma Asokaraja, the ruler of Sukhothai, that he intended to go to Satchanalai. After arriving in Satchanalai he told King Lithai all about the Buddha relic [so that the king would help him] remove the relic. Upon hearing this news, the king of Satchanalai was overjoyed and donated a labor force to help dig up the relic. Mahasumana Thera took the group to the city of Bangcha and built a wooden altar for offerings of puffed rice, flowers, and scented water in order to worship the virtuous qualities of the Buddha. That night Mahasumana ascended the altar where he asked the relic to perform a miracle. The monk saw the needle flower bush in the shape of a stool and at the same time observed the Buddha relic miraculously multiplying itself in the shape of small crabs. Mahasumana quickly had some of the workmen make a banner to mark the site. The Buddha relic continued to perform miracles all night long.

The next day, Mahasumana ordered all the workmen to take the five or eight precepts before digging a hole first through dirt and then stones. After that they continued to dig until they found the casket that encased the relic. Mahasumana raised it up and saw that the outermost covering was brass, the second was silver, the third gold, and the innermost casket was crystal the size of a pomegranate. Everyone wondered if this was the relic or a coral because there was no place to open it. Mahasumana said, "This is not the Buddha relic. It is only a container. Let us make offerings to the Buddha." Mahasumana Thera then presented offerings of flowers and sweetly scented water, and prayed. [At that moment] the Thera saw an opening in the crystal casket. After opening it he saw a Buddha relic the size of a pea shining like gold.

Mahasumana Thera lustrated the relic with scented water and made many offerings to it. The relic miraculously divided into two, three, and finally eight relics floating around on the water. It was so astonishing that every part of Mahasumana's body tingled as though he was seeing the Buddha himself when he was still alive.[10] Then Mahasumana Thera reported the discovery of the eight precious relics to the king of Satchanalai. When the king heard the news, he was exceedingly glad and ordered the construction of a golden pavilion. That night he invited the Buddha [relic] [to enter the golden pavilion]. As Mahasumana was making offerings to the relic, it performed many miracles in full view of everyone. When the king of Satchanalai saw the Buddha relic he worshipped it and sent messengers to inform the King of Sukhothai, Siridhammaraja who was overjoyed and thought, "The Buddha relic will perform miracles for me and when it does I shall build a golden *chedi* in my city in order to worship it."

The king of Sukhothai then invited the Buddha [relic] and Mahasumana Thera to the city where he presented many offerings to the Lord's relic and lustrated it with water. However, the Buddha relic performed no miracles for him because Sukhothai was deemed an unsuitable location for the Buddha relic. When Dhammaraja, the king of Sukhothai, saw that the Buddha relic did not perform miracles he lost faith in it and returned the relic to Mahasumana Thera to maintain and protect. Mahasumana respectfully made many offerings to the Buddha relic and continued to perform his monastic duties in Sukhothai and Satchanalai for a long time. Here ends the third chapter that relates the story of Sumana Thera receiving the skull bone relic (*matthalungadhatu*) [of the Buddha].[11]

The Buddha Relic and Sumana Thera Arrive in Chiang Mai

Once there was a king named, Kue Na, who ruled in Chiang Mai. When he heard about the fame of Udumbara Mahaswami at the city of Martaban, King Kue Na sent a delegation to invite the Mahaswami to come to Chiang Mai. The Mahaswami refused the invitation but sent ten of his disciples, headed by Ananda Thera, to go in his stead. King Kue Na invited them to stay at the Lokaphai Monastery and requested that they carry out such monastic responsibilities as ordination. The monks replied, "O king, Udumbara Mahaswami asked us to come here in order that your merit might increase, however, we are forbidden to conduct [such] monastic duties [as ordination]. Udumbara Mahaswami's disciple, Mahasumana Thera by name, can propagate Buddhism in Siam. At present Mahasumana is teaching in Sukhothai. O king, you should invite him here. When he arrives, all of us with Mahasumana Thera will be able to conduct the full range of monastic duties." Then King Kue Na sent his minister, Muen Ngoen Kong, with two white-robed renunciants named Yot and Sai, to Sukhothai to invite Mahasumana Thera. Mahasumana told Ananda, his disciple, to assume his duties at Wat Pa Kaeo. Subsequently, Mahasumana went [to Chiang Mai] with his nephew, a novice named Kumarakassapa, who was nearly twenty years old. King Kue Na was overjoyed to learn that Mahasumana had accepted his invitation. The king with his retinue went to receive Mahasumana, who was almost sixty years old, at a place called Saen Khao Ho and led him to Wat Phra Yuen, east of the city of Lamphun. This was in the year *kat rao*, C.S. 731 (1369 C.E.). King Kue Na invited Mahasumana to conduct monastic duties

Statue of the elephant that carried the Buddha relic to the summit of Doi Suthep, Wat Phra That Doi Suthep

such as ordination and to establish boundary markers. Mahasumana Thera together with ten other Mahathera monks sent by Udumbara-pupphamahaswami ordained Kumarakassapa in the Mae Raming [Mae Ping] River at Wat Candabhanu.[12] King Kue Na was pleased with the virtuous behavior of Mahasumana Thera and conferred on him the title, Sumanapuppharatana Mahaswami.

One day Mahasumana displayed the relic to King Kue Na for him to venerate and related its history from the time that the gods told him about the relic in a dream. Greatly moved by the sight of the relic, King Kue Na poured lustral water over the gold casket in which it was kept. Then the relic miraculously multiplied by twos and threes, half of them were golden in color and the other half the color of an alloy of gold and copper. They floated clockwise on the water. That same day a heavy rain fell out of season. Upon witnessing this miracle, King Kue Na and his officials were exceedingly glad and exclaimed, "Satthu, Satthu."

Mahasumana Thera stayed at Wat Phra Yuen for two years. In the year *kot set*, c.s.. 732 (1370 c.e.) towards the end of the year, King Kue Na told his ministers to build a monastery in his pleasure gardens filled with plumeria trees and name it Wat Suan Dok Mai Luang [Royal Flower Garden Monastery]. When it was finished he sent an emissary to invite Mahasumana to be the abbot in the year *ruang kai*, c.s. 733 (1371 c.e.). In this year, King Kue Na had Mahasumana build a large *chedi* at Wat Suan Dok in order to enshrine the Buddha relic. Afterwards they put the relic into a golden bowl over which they poured consecrated water. The relic performed a miracle for King Kue Na, Mahasumana Thera, and all of the people, dividing into twos and threes and floating clockwise on the water. Some were of a golden color, some the color of an alloy of gold and copper, some the color of pearl, and others the color of coral. At the same time the sky miraculously darkened. King Kue Na and his retinue including commoners, Brahmans, and monks were amazed and delighted. They raised their hands over their heads to pay respects to the relic and exclaimed, "Satthu, Satthu." When Mahasumana Thera removed the Buddha relic from the water in the golden container, it had coalesced into two parts. They were equally beautiful but one was smaller than the other. The division of the relic occurred because of King Kue Na's and Mahasumana's powerful resolve. They then put the larger relic with the appearance of coral into four caskets that fit inside of one another, the smallest [containing the relic] being gold, the next silver, then an alloy of gold and copper, and finally clay. This was enshrined in the *chedi* at Wat Suan Dok Mai Luang so that everyone—human beings and gods—could venerate it for five thousand years. Here ends the fourth chapter of the enshrinement of the Buddha relic at Wat Suan Dok Mai Luang.[13]

The Buddha Relic Enshrined on Doi Suthep

In the year *ruang kai*, c.s. 733 (1371 c.e.), King Kue Na and Mahasumana Thera decided to enshrine the second Buddha relic in another place, saying, "When the appropriate place is discovered, we shall enshrine the relic there. Let us adorn an auspicious elephant with gold trappings. Then we shall place the Buddha relic in a crystal casket filigreed with gold and place it on the elephant's back under a white umbrella and a royal fan." [After the relic was prepared in this way] a variety of musical instruments were played and the relic was blessed with puffed rice, flowers, and scented water. King Kue Na and Mahasumana prayed to all the divine beings, "O gods, you who guard the earth, please lead the elephant to an auspicious place where the Buddha relic will be enshrined so that all human beings and gods may worship the relic for five thousand years." Then as it trumpeted, the elephant was released. Accompanied by music, Kue Na, Mahasumana, and their retinue followed it. The elephant trumpeted three times and then left through the city gate in the direction of Doi Suthep. When it came to the foot of a mountain, King Kue Na and Mahasumana thought that the elephant would stop there. However, it only knelt down but refused to stay there and continued on its way. This place was called the mountain where the elephant knelt down (Doi Chang Non). Later it was called Jackfruit Mountain (Doi Makkhanun) by which it is still known today. The elephant continued walking toward the top of the mountain. King Kue Na and Mahasumana, spying a lovely, level place, thought that the Buddha relic should be enshrined there. They invited the relic [to come down from the back of the elephant], but again the elephant refused to stop and continued on its way. This place was called the Beautiful Field on Top of the Mountain (Sanam Yot Ngam). Later it was given the name, the Lovely Three Peaks (Sam Yot Ngam) and has been called this name until today. The elephant continued its ascent until it came to the summit of Doi Suthep whereupon it trumpeted three times and thrice circumambulated. Then, at that very spot it knelt on its four legs.

King Kue Na was delighted and arranged for music to be played to pay respects to [the relic] while everyone shouted, "Satthu, Satthu," in a loud cacophony of sound. King Kue Na and Mahasumana Thera requested that the Buddha relic come down from the back of the elephant. Immediately, after the relic was removed from its back, the elephant died on the top of the mountain. King Kue Na and Mahasumana Thera had a hole dug three cubits deep, made a large crypt out of six stone slabs for the four sides, top and bottom, and then placed the relic casket in it. Afterwards they filled the hole with

Statue of Khruba Siwichai who inspired the construction of the road up Doi Suthep to Wat Phra That

stones level with the ground before making a *chedi* over it twenty meters in height in order that human beings and gods could venerate it. This was done in c.s. 733 (1371 c.e.).

Another *tamnan* says that King Kue Na enshrined three Buddha relics before c.s. 748 (1386 c.e.) on the full moon day of Visakha, a Friday in the year *kap chai*, the sixteenth of November. Chapter five of the enshrinement of the relic on Doi Suthep is now finished.[14]

Kings of Chiang Mai and Wat Phra That Doi Suthep

From the time King Mangrai founded the city of Chiang Mai in c.s. 658 (1296 c.e.), the year *rawai san* until King Kue Na and Mahasumana Thera enshrined the relic in the forest of Suthep in the year c.s. 733 (1371 c.e.), a period of seventy-five years, five kings ruled the city. King Mangrai ruled Chiang Mai for twenty-eight years before he died.[15] Then, his nephew, Saen Phu ruled for twenty-nine years. His son, Kham Fu, reigned for eight years. His son, Pha Yu, ruled for twenty-two years. His son, Kue Na assumed the throne in the year *moeng met*, c.s. 729 (1367 c.e.) until the year *ruang kai*, c.s. 733 (1371 c.e.). He enshrined the Buddha relic in the forest of Suthep Mountain. In the year *moeng mao*, c.s. 749 (1387 c.e.), his son, Saen Mueng Ma, ruled in Chiang Mai for fifteen years. His son, Sam Fang Kaen, ruled for forty-two years. His son, Tilokarat ruled for forty-six years. His nephew, Yot Chiang Rai, ruled for nine years. His son, Thao Kaeo, ruled for thirty-one years.

All the kings who ruled in Chiang Mai from King Kue Na to Thao Kaeo placed great faith in the Buddha relic on Suthep Mountain and continuously made offerings to it. The son of Thao Kaeo, named Thao Ai, became king in the year *dap rao*, c.s. 887 (1525 c.e.). He also had great faith in the Buddha relic and invited Maha Nanamangalabodhi from Wat Asoka Arama to supervise the building of a large *chedi* [on Doi Suthep] in the year *poek set*, c.s. 900 (1538 c.e.), the eighth month, on a Thursday the thirteenth day of the waxing moon. The square base of the large *chedi* was twelve cubits wide and forty-four cubits high. At each of the four corners were vases for golden lotuses. The hexagonal pedestal above the base was four meters high, and it was decorated with lotus petals pointing down from the top and up from the bottom in two rows in an overlapping triangular design that resembled a snake's backbone in-between. The round top was crowned by a golden lotus and filigreed with jewels.

In the year *rawai san*, c.s. 898 (1536 c.e.), Thao Chai, the son of Thao Ai, became the king of Chiang Mai. He contributed a seventeen-hundred-baht weight of gold for gilding the *chedi* and six thousand in cash to construct a chapel. In the year *ka mao*, c.s. 905 (1543 c.e.). Mahananamangalabodhi built two chapels at the front and the back of the *chedi* and a veranda enclosure covered with beautiful murals. In the year *moeng sai*, c.s. 919 (1557 c.e.). Mahananamangalabodhi supervised the building of a large staircase flanked by two Nagas on the left and right. Thus ends the sixth chapter that relates the construction of the *mahachedi*.

The Temple on Suthep Mountain and Its Veneration[16]

The base of the *mahachedi* is twelve meters on each side for a total of forty-eight meters. The iron fence surrounding the *chedi* is fourteen meters on each side for a total of fifty-six meters. The fence on the east has one hundred twenty-eight iron bars, on the south one hundred thirty-two, on the west one hundred thirty-three, and on the north one hundred twenty, making a total of five hundred and thirteen. On each corner is a tower. Around each side are candela-bras eighteen meters in length for a total of seventy-two meters. There are twenty-eight golden oil lamps on the east and twenty-seven on the west, north, and south for a total of one hundred and nine. There are forty-seven rooms for monks surrounding the *chedi*.

The boundary from north to south is thirty-eight meters and from east to west forty-four meters. It is eighteen meters from the entrance to the guardian deities and one hundred forty meters to the Naga at the bottom of one hundred seventy-three steps. The wooden fence from west to east is one hundred meters and eighty meters from south to north.

In those days a layman named Mangalasila sponsored the building of an ordination hall. He was told by a deity [in a dream] that formerly the place had been the site for ordinations during the time of previous Buddhas. The abbot of Wat Suan Dok was asked to consecrate it. Whenever the future Buddha, Phra Ariya Metteya, appears he will reside in the ordination hall. Doi Suthep is so highly esteemed that every Buddha of this eon has come to the mountain.[17]

King Phra Mueang Kaeo sent monks to study Buddhism in Burma (Ava) accompanied by ambassadors. The ruler of Ava asked, "Have you ever gone to worship the Buddha relic on Doi Suthep." The ambassadors [replied that they had] and asked the king why he was so unfortunate [that he had not had such an opportunity]."

From this time forth, all the Buddha relics that are not protected by a deity will come together at Doi Suthep. After five thousand years, they will enter base of the Bodhi tree [under which the Buddha was enlightened].[18] Everyone who worships the Buddha relic at Doi Suthep is worshipping the living Buddha.

There was a Sangharat at Hongsawadi who asked the monks from Chiang Mai if they had ever worshipped the Buddha relic on Doi Suthep. Those who had, answered that they had worshipped the Buddha relic [on Doi Suthep]. [Because of this act of veneration] the Sangharat offered monastic robes to them saying, "All of the relics will come together in the *chedi* on Doi Suthep. Therefore, all the human and divine beings and who pay respects to the Buddha relic and make offerings there do so to the living Buddha himself."

There was a man, Muen La by name, who had never worshipped the Suthep Buddha relic but, when he overheard the remarks made by the Hongsawadi monks, he was so inspired [by this information] that he removed a gold bracelet from his wrist and handed it over to a goldsmith to make into a plaque to put on the Doi Suthep *chedi* as an offering. He related what he had been told by the monks of Hongsawadi about the Buddhas and the relic on Doi Suthep and praised the Buddhas throughout time for their surpassing worth for all humankind. All men and women should pay their respects to the Doi Suthep *chedi* by joining their hands together [before the *chedi*] and make offerings of flowers, sandalwood powder, and fragrant objects, or of silver and gold, clothing, jewelry, and food and recall the virtues of the Buddhas with the following verse, "The Blessed One is the Perfected One, the Fully Enlightened Buddha," and keep this verse in mind while silently circumambulating the relic.

Thus ends the story of the Buddha relic on Doi Suthep. This verse was uttered by the *arahant* monks who realized nirvana [not only for themselves but] as an encouragement for those considering becoming a monk to do so with a firm faith and for the purpose of remaining in the monkhood for their entire life.[19] This verse is not to be taken lightly.

Concluding Summary

The author of the text uses the verse as a transition to a long sermon on what it means to be a good monk and engage in serious monastic practice. To pursue nirvana brings a greater happiness than returning to lay life to enjoy the pleasures of the world. Monks who withdraw from the world and practice meditation are freed from the pressures that accompany lay life. The pursuit of worldly goals leaves no time for meditation. The author includes in his discourse a dialogue attributed to the Buddha and stories that focus on punishment for evil actions and the decline of Buddhism that will be followed by the appearance of Phra Ariya Metteya, the future Buddha. At the end of this section the author recounts in a random order the highlights of Buddhist history including events in the life of the Buddha, the monastic councils, King Asoka, the coming of Buddhism to Sri Lanka, Buddhaghosa, Buddhism's arrival in Hariphunchai, Aniruddha's establishment of the Chulasakarat calendar, King Mangrai and the beginning the Chiang Mai dynasty, the kingdom of Ayutthaya, and the Burmese occupation of northern Thailand.

The concluding colophon notes that the *tamnan* was copied in c.s. 1186 (1824 c.e.).

THE LEGEND OF DOI KHAM. THE GOLDEN MOUNTAIN

Phra That Doi Kham in the Time of the Buddha

Once upon a time about nineteen years after the Buddha's enlightenment when he was fifty years old, the Blessed One thought, "After I have passed away, human beings in different countries will suffer moral defilements and will not know my teaching (dharma). I will show compassion on those people far and wide who are mired in worldly desires in order to save them from disaster. They shall be the foundation for my law for future generations."

After this reflection, the Blessed One journeyed north together with the *arahant* monks and Indra. Whenever he saw a town where the people were mired in moral defilement he endeavored to teach them the dharma so they might be released from suffering. Whenever the people of a particular town became followers of

1986 Bangkok Post *cartoon ridiculing the proposed construction of a cable car to Wat Phra That Doi Suthep*

the Buddha, he left a footprint and a relic for them and future generations to venerate.

The Blessed One and all the *arahant* monks carried on their training without ceasing even when wandering was very difficult and filled with obstacles. The Blessed One traveled on until he reached the city of Burapha and from there continued north where he stopped in a village (today this place is Wat Chedi Liam). From there he continued west to Doi Kham where three Yakkhas resided—a father, mother, and their child. The three ate the meat of humans and animals that they frequently caught and consumed. When they saw the Lord Buddha approaching together with his disciples they were intent on capturing and eating them as was their custom. The Lord Buddha, knowing their nature, extended loving-kindness to them and by the power of his great merit prevented their defilement from arising. Each of the three Yakkhas, the father, Chikham [also known as Pu Sae], the mother, Ta Khiao [also known as Ya Sae], and the child [Wasuthep], fearful of the Buddha's extraordinary spiritual powers, prostrated at his feet. The Lord Buddha extended compassion to the three Yakkhas and thought, "These three have fallen to a lowly fate because of their past evil deeds, but in the future after my death they will follow my teaching." Because of this foreknowledge he preached a sermon to tame their evil nature. The Yakkhas promised to follow the Buddha's rules (*vinaya*) but Chikham and Ta Khiao were unable to keep the five precepts all of the time. They asked the Buddha if they could eat the flesh of two sentient beings once a year. The Buddha granted the request but only on the condition that it was the flesh of an animal, not a human being. He also ordered the two Yakkhas to seek permission from the village headman to pass by his village. He did so because it was far better for the Yakkhas to eat the flesh of animals rather than humans. For this reason there came to be a ceremony whereby a white buffalo was slaughtered for Pu Sae and a black buffalo for Ya Sae but they are given only the ears. The ceremony for Pu Sae is held at Wat Fai Hin [located at the foot of Doi Suthep] and for Ya Sae at the foot of Doi Kham. (This custom is still observed.)

The Yakkha child also requested permission to become the Buddha's disciple and the Blessed One agreed. On this occasion the Buddha preached a sermon and gave Pu Sae and Ya Sae a hair relic saying, "Receive this relic and take great care of it. In the future it will be venerated in my stead. Two thousand years after my death many people of great merit will gather here." The two Yakkhas accepted the Lord Buddha's relic, enshrined it in an emerald casket, and constantly worshipped it. After that a miracle occurred. For three days and nights a gold-like rain fell and flowed into the cave [where the relic was kept] so that it was called the "Golden Cave." Subsequently, the Buddha placed one of his footprints on a stone under a plumeria tree to the east of Doi Kham. The stone, guarded by a deity, then disappeared into the ground to appear in the future for the benefit of humans everywhere.

The Yakkha youth did not remain a monk for long before he requested permission to leave the Buddha's order of monks to become

Pu Sae and Ya Sae, Wat Phra That Doi Kham

an ascetic. The Buddha gave his permission and named the ascetic Wasuthep or Thewaruesi. From that time forth the [buffalo] sacrifice to appease the spirits of Pu Sae and Ya Sae has been held on the full moon day of the seventh month according to the northern Thai reckoning.

After Pu Sae and Ya Sae died, the relic enshrined in the cave on Doi Kham was maintained by Wasuthep and then, subsequently, by Queen Chama after she became the ruler of Hariphunchai. Here follows the story of Queen Chama.

Phra That Doi Kham during the Time of Chamathewi

A wealthy man and his wife once lived in the neighborhood of Ban Nongkhu, Pasang district in the province of Lamphun. They were very good friends with another wealthy couple. Because of their deep mutual affection the couples agreed that if they had children they should marry. Before long one couple had a baby girl and the other a baby boy. They were delighted at the thought of becoming even closer [through the marriage of their children]. However, because of the exceptional virtue of the female child, she was destined to grow up to be the leader of northern Thailand (Lan Na). Therefore, it was

Spirit medium (ma-khi) *at buffalo sacrifice. Ban Hiya, Doi Kham, 1994*

inappropriate for her to enter into a previously arranged marriage. To be a queen she required instruction by a qualified teacher in order to be able to govern in the future.

One day when the baby girl was three months old she fell asleep outside of the house. A large hawk chieftain flew by who spied the child and considering her a tasty meal, swooped down, and seized the baby in its talons. The hawk immediately flew up into the sky to the northwest so no one could rescue the baby. Coincidentally, at the same time the hawk was flying over Doi Kham Mountain, Wasuthep set about to honor the ashes of his parents, Pu Sae and Ya Sae. The ascetic saw the hawk clutching the baby in its talons, and knew that the young child had been stolen and would be killed. Calming his mind, Wasuthep rebuked the hawk. His powerful appearance so frightened the bird that it released the baby and it floated down to the earth toward a pond on Doi Kham Mountain. Miraculously, the petals of a large lotus in the pond opened to receive the child and prevented her from drowning. Wasuthep was amazed at this occurrence. He stood with his fan, approached the child and prayed, "If this child is to be a person of great meritorious accomplishment in the future, may she float up to this fan." The child then floated toward Wasuthep's fan just as he had prayed. Because of this event Wasuthep named the child, Fan (*wi*).[20]

During the time that Chama was a child [under the care of Wasuthep] the chief of the Lawa, Wilangkha, and the chief of the Thai Yai [Shan], Chao Luang Kham Daeng, were constantly at war. [To resolve their differences], Wasuthep called a meeting between Wilangkha and Chao Luang Kham Daeng on Doi Kham. At that time the Thai Yai wore trousers only to their knees while the Lawa cut their hair and wore trousers twisted from the front through the knees and tied in the back. At the meeting it was agreed that the Thai Yai would wear their hair like the Lawa and the Lawa would wear trousers like the Thai Yai. From that time forth there was no more warfare between the Lawa and the Thai Yai and they lived together peacefully.

Wasuthep attentively cared for the child, teaching her the arts and sciences. When she was thirteen years old, he made a raft out of bamboo, furnished it with provisions and prayed, "If this young girl is to be a person of great future accomplishment and a ruler of a kingdom, may this raft float there. May no harm come to her nor may any danger befall her." Having made this resolve, Wasuthep set the raft afloat on the Raming River (the river Ping that flows through Chiang Mai). The lithesome, teenage girl floated down the river unafraid of the forces of nature because she had been taught by Wasuthep not to be afraid or apprehensive when faced with danger. Indeed, it was quite the opposite. During the journey through an isolated, distant land the girl rejoiced in nature and was a friend to all of the various forest animals she passed by. Finally she arrived at the city of Lawo, an area governed by the Khom [Khmer], where the raft came to rest at the pier of the cloister at Wat Chueng Tha that was used by the king whenever he went boating on the river. The people of the city were amazed when they saw that the raft had come to rest at the pier because ordinarily the river's current was so strong that only the king was able to land there. When the king, Chao Noppharat, was told what had happened he went to the pier and saw for himself that, indeed, a raft had come to rest there with a beautiful girl on board who possessed the traits of a person of great merit. The king raised her as his adopted daughter and gave her the name, Chamathewi. He cared for her until she was twenty-four years old when she was married to his viceroy, the ruler of the city of Ramapuri, a Khmer outpost (the district of Mae Sot in the province of Tak). Later the king sent Chamathewi to govern Hariphunchai in response to the request of the ascetics, Wasuthep and Suthanta. They said, "Chamathewi is beautiful beyond comparison and wiser than any man. O, King Noppharat, please favor us by making Chamathewi the ruler of Hariphunchai. Chamathewi's beauty is known far and wide: her mouth is shaped like an egg; her hair as black as the feathers of a cormorant; her dark eyes are radiant with joy; her eyebrows curve like a hunter's bent bow. She has a large nose, distinctive facial features, lips as red as vermilion, teeth as beautifully smooth, white, and pure as a pearl. Her elbows are plump; her waist as slender as an elephant's trunk; her body as sweet smelling as a lotus and so graceful when she walks that she looks like a swan moving on water. In all Lan Na no one can equal her grace and beauty. She is truly beyond description."

Chamathewi became the ruler of Hariphunchai and after Wasuthep's death guarded the relic and treasure hidden in the Doi Kham cave. Chamathewi had two sons, Mahantayot and Annatayot [who subsequently ruled Hariphunchai/Lamphun and Khelangkha/Lampang]. The chronicles attest to the queen's superlative qualities. She built many temples and monasteries wherever she went in

Hariphunchai (Lamphun province). The many *wat*s she had constructed include Wat Chamathewi, Wat Kulamak, Wat Chang Kham, Wat Mahawan, Wat Phra Yuen, Wat Lawo, Wat Phra Khong Ruesi, Wat Pratu Li, Wat Phra That Doi Kham, Wat Phra That Doi Noi as well as many *wat*s in other provinces.

Chamathewi's beauty so infatuated Wilangkha that he sent a royal letter to Hariphunchai inviting her to be his queen. Finding his proposal repugnant, Chamathewi devised a clever stratagem [to reject Wilangkha's offer of marriage]. She sent a royal message in reply, requesting that Wilangkha prove his strength before the people in order to demonstrate that he would be a suitable husband. Because at that time Wilangkha was very powerful and had a large army, Chamathewi did not want to risk a war so she challenged him, saying, "If my lord has the strength to hurl a spear [from the top of Doi Suthep] to the city of Hariphunchai [a distance of about thirty kilometers], I shall agree to be your queen." Wilangkha was very strong and was an expert spearsman so he accepted Chamathewi's challenge to throw his spear from the top of Suthep Mountain twice within a fifteen-day period.[21] On his first try, the soldier Chamathewi had posted as an observer reported that the spear almost reached the boundary of the city. Alarmed, she thought of a way to address the situation. She made a beautiful garland of flowers but put a magic *mantra* in it [to sap Wilangkha's strength].[22] She then had her minister present the garland to Wilangkha with the message, "I am impressed at the great distance you threw your spear, nearly reaching my city. When you hurl your spear again, please wear this garland of flowers as a reminder that my heart is with you." Wilangkha was delighted. Spellbound by the thought of Chamathewi's love, he put the garland around his neck when he threw the spear the second time. But the power of the *mantra*, weakened him and he failed.

Wilangkha felt very confident when the first spear nearly reached Hariphunchai. Why had his second throw traveled so short a distance that it seemed to disappear? When he realized that the second spear only reached to Doi Lek at the edge of Doi Suthep just north of Doi Kham in his own territory, he knew that Chamathewi had bested him. (Today villagers call the place the Ascetic's Well). Realizing that Chamathewi did not love him and that there was no hope of marriage, Wilangkha decided to seize Hariphunchai by force so he raised an army and attacked the city. The army of Hariphunchai immediately prepared to counterattack. Chamathewi appointed her two sons as commanders of the army. Mahantayot led the charge riding on an elephant of supernatural power. The chronicle relates the following story about the elephant.

Early in Chamathewi's reign, she heard about a silvery white elephant with green tusks living at the base of Doi Ang Salung (in the Chiang Dao district). With many offerings and musicians she set out to invite the large, auspicious animal to reside in her royal elephant stable so that she could care for and honor it. It was quite apparent that the elephant was invested with extraordinary power. Because of its appearance, the people called the animal "The Elephant with the Dark Green Tusks."

The queen's two sons mounted the elephant, the younger in the back, and went forth at the head of the army to confront Wilangkha on elephant back. The elephant's power was so astonishing that the chieftain was frightened to death when the tusks of the two elephants interlocked. According to the chronicle, when that happened flames shot out from the green tusks of Mahantayot's elephant causing Wilangkha to turn and flee. Upon witnessing this event, the will of the Lawa forces to fight evaporated and they beat a pell mell retreat. With the defeat of the Lawa army, Chamathewi's fame spread in all directions.

Having become the custodian of the place occupied by her foster father, Wasuthep, Chamathewi appointed her two sons to build a small *chedi* on the summit of Doi Kham. There she enshrined a crystal casket in which a hair relic of the Buddha had been placed and repeated the words the Blessed One had taught Wasuthep that he, in turn, had passed on to her: "Until that time arrives for the appearance of the Buddha's relics when many people of great merit will gather together, evil and degenerate people should never build temples or monasteries or take the precepts. If they do, these places will disappear due to the power of the Buddha's prediction. For a long period of time, whenever one builds a monastery it will be destroyed and abandoned. Even if a pious, faithful person restores it, in a short time it will be abandoned again."

According to the Buddha's prediction, twenty-five hundred years after the Buddha's death, this relic [on Doi Kham] will flourish because it will be venerated by all the people. [Following the Buddha's prediction], at the present time the *chedi* on Doi Kham is being restored. As the history of Doi Kham reveals, it is one of the keys to Chiang Mai.

RECOVERING THE PAST TO GAIN A FUTURE

Nearly three decades ago I recall Achan Sommai describing to me his life as a child of rice farmers in the northeast. He grew up in a rural area just before Thailand's transformation into an increasingly urbanized, industrialized, modernized country. I was amazed at the extent of his knowledge that revealed an intimate relationship with animals and nature. He was familiar with the names of all the birds, insects, trees, and plants and saw his water buffalo as a close friend. But more than names, all had stories—some originating from Sommai's personal experience in the village and its environs, while others were an inherited lore passed on by elders.

The rural past of Achan Sommai's childhood largely has vanished, and some would say, "well and good." Thais enjoy most of the benefits of modernization—electricity, cleaner water, better health services, and so on—as does much of the world. But while the life of a rural farmer fifty or sixty years ago was far from idyllic and should not be overly romanticized, its connections to nature and to community, a sense of place and the stories that narrate its history often are sacrificed to a life that may be richer in material things but poorer in a meaningful connection to the natural world.

I am interested in the stories of Doi Ang Salung Chiang Dao, Doi Suthep, and Doi Kham as handed down from the past because of their inherent appeal as a work of northern Thai culture. My interest is not merely academic, however. I believe that such stories are more than cultural artifacts; they have the power to guide the present and promote a wiser, more empathetic lifestyle that honors and celebrates nature.

Few twenty-first-century Thais actually believe that the Buddha visited northern Thailand or that Chao Luang Kham Daeng was transformed into a guardian Yakkha in the Chiang Dao cave. However, these narratives ascribe to Lan Na a sacredness it would otherwise lack, and like any good story, they have the power to fire the imagination and the commitment of those who love Chiang Mai's mountains as a work of nature and of culture. Pu Sae, Ya Sae, Wasuthep, Wilangkha, Chamathewi, and the Buddha consecrated these mountains. Now it is our turn to protect them.

NOTES

Chapter I Buddhism, Nature, and Culture

1. See *Bangkok Post*, Monday, November 13, 1989, "EGAT Warns of Low Water Level in Dams," pp. 1, 3.

2. For example, see Francesca Bray, "Agriculture for Developing Nations," *Scientific American*, July 1994; D. Pimentel, et al, "Benefits and Risks of Genetic Engineering in Agriculture," *Bioscience*, vol. 39, no. 10 (1989).

3. Paraphrased from a lecture delivered at the McGilvary Theological Faculty of Payap University on October 27, 1989 ("Kwam Khaochai Kiaokap Sangkhom Thai: Khabuankan Chai Amnat lae Kanyaek Chiwit Ok Pen Suan" [Understanding Thai Society: Violence and Alienation].

4. The first issue of *Generation* (October, 1989), an expensive, elitist magazine contained a lead article, "The Buddha's Tears. The Decline of Buddhism in Thailand" ("Namtatthakhot: Anicca Phutthasasana nai Mueng Thai)," 39–55. In the article some of the more important voices for reform of the Thai Sangha and Thai society were mentioned, including Buddhadasa and Sulak Sivaraksa.

5. Buddhadasa Bhikkhu, Phutthasasanik Kap Kan Anurak Thammachat [Buddhists and the Care of Nature] (Bangkok: Komol Kimthong Foundation, 1990), 35. Translation by the author. The comparison between Buddhadasa's vision and similar ecological visions in other religious traditions is striking. For example, see Ernesto Cardenal, "To Live is to Love," in *Silent Fire: An Invitation to Western Mysticism*, ed. Walter Holden Capps and Wendy M. Wright (New York: Harper and Row, Publishers), 1978.

6. Buddhadasa Bhikkhu, Siang Takon Jak Thammachat [Shouts from Nature] (Bangkok: Sublime Life Mission, 1971), 5–7 Translation by the author.

7. Ibid., 7.

8. Ibid., 15–16.

9. Nancy Nash, "The Buddhist Perception of Nature Project," in Buddhist Perspectives on the Ecocrisis, ed. Klas Sandell, The Wheel, vol. 18 (Kandy, Sri Lanka: Buddhist Publication Society, 1987), 73.

Chapter II Mountains and Sacred Space

1. It is customary to erect long banners or flags (*tung*) at a wide variety of northern Thai Buddhist merit-making ceremonies. The custom is also practiced among the Shan and the Lao. Generally it is said that the length of the flag provides an opportunity for those being punished in the Buddhist hells to grab the tail of the banner and thus escape from their karmic punishment; that is, the power of the merit generated by the ritual produces a beneficent effect for the dead as well as the living.

2. A possible reference to Wat Chedi Luang, in Pali Jotikarama, a major Chiang Mai monastery associated with the rulers of Chiang Mai.

3. Wat Chom Thong south of Chiang Mai is a highly revered pilgrimage site. The reliquary there is in a pyramidal form.

4. Chao Luang Kham Daeng is the guardian spirit of Chiang Dao. He is the functional equivalent of Pu Sae/Ya Sae, the Lawa guardian spirits of the Doi Suthep/Doi Kham area adjacent to the city of Chiang Mai.

5. In the conclusion of the text we are reminded that relatively brief *Buddha tamnan*, such as *Tamnan Ang Salung*, were originally preached texts. Presumably they originated as oral texts and were eventually written on palm leaves.

6. Popular Buddhist devotion in Thailand today is often limited to this magical, instrumentalist understanding of the Buddha and lacks the more profound levels of interpretation embodied in the *Buddha tamnan*.

7. Conventionally, "naming" within the context of folklore is given an etiological significance, that is, why a place is named such and such. While there is an etiological signification to naming in the *tamnan*, I am suggesting an additional deeper, cosmological meaning that creates order and meaning in the manner of a cosmological map.

8. *Rueang Lao Chaokhun Pho* [Chaokhun Pho Talks about Various Matters] (Chiang Mai: Center for the Preservation of Arts and Culture, Chiang Mai University, B.E. 2542/C.E. 1999).

Chapter III Doi Ang Salung: Water Basin Mountain

1. Rather than a literal rendering of the text, the translators have attempted to convey the meaning of the story. Even though some ambiguities remain unresolved, we hope no blatant errors have been introduced, and that our work makes a modest contribution to the study of the Buddha-chronicle (*Buddha tamnan*) tradition, now only in its infancy. For a study of Phra That

Doi Tung see Hans Penth, *Prawati Phra That Doi Tung. History of Phra That Doi Tung* (Bangkok/Chiang Rai: Mae Fah Luang Foundation, 1993).

2.   Translated by Donald K. Swearer and Phaithoon Dokbuakaew.

3.   Located in the district of Hot, Chiang Mai province. A relic is enshrined on the mountain. The Buddha's travels, which occupy a significant portion of this chronicle, are similar to the account in the ninth palm-leaf bundle of the northern Thai chronicle known as the *Buddha Tamnan*. The format of the various legends of the Buddha's visit to northern Thailand follow a similar pattern. In this genre of *tamnan*, whether an account of one or of many sites, the Buddha's actual presence legitimates them as places worthy of veneration.

4.   Distances given in *wa* are converted to meters. In this case 10,000 *wa* equal 20,000 meters. Distances, heights, and depths are often highly exaggerated suggesting the mythic-legendary nature of the story.

5.   The Lawa were an indigenous people who inhabited northern Thailand prior to Tai migrations into the area from the thirteenth century. Hariphunchai was a major Mon-Lawa cultural center.

6.   In the chronicle literature it is common for a monk accompanying the Buddha to be referred to by the generic term, *arahant*, "worthy one." It represents the highest stage of spiritual attainment. The term is often simply rendered as "monk."

7.   Popular chronicles such as the Legend of Water Basin Mountain are fundamentally mythic in nature. The primary purpose of the chronicle is to convey the normative belief in the sacralizing presence of the Buddha in northern Thailand, rather than relating a historically accurate account. Consequently, the text ignores such rational questions as how the Buddha and his monks could have traveled to northern Thailand, or how King Asoka (third century B.C.E.) could appear on the same historical stage with the Buddha.

8.   Lay membership in Thai Theravada tradition does not require a formal initiation ritual as is the case in most Christian and Jewish traditions such as baptism, confirmation, or *bar mitzvah*. Perhaps the closest approximation of lay "membership" in the Buddhist community is "taking the five precepts." Thai Buddhist ritual occasions always begin with the laity paying respects to the triple gem (the Buddha, the Dharma, and the Sangha), and then requesting the five precepts—not to take the life of sentient beings, not to steal, not to commit adultery, not to lie, not consume intoxicants. When the Lawa "took the precepts" they became followers of the Buddha.

9. "Popular" Buddhism has a prudential or pragmatic character. The Buddhist precepts are a guide to ethical behavior not divine commandments. Sanctions are calculated in terms of karmic consequences, meritorious or demeritorious. In this episode "taking the precepts" has the prudential meaning of resulting in material benefits rather than following a set of moral precepts on the way to the goal of nirvana.

10. Tathagata ("thus-gone") refers to the Buddha's achievement of transcending the wheel of rebirth and, thus, to have "gone" to the further shore of Nirvana. Since the term is not easily translated, I simply use it as a title or designation for the Buddha.

11. Hot means a place that is dry, has little water. Indeed, even today the district of Hot is a dry region. Etiologies are an important element in popular chronicles such as the Legend of Water Basin Mountain. In northern Thai *tamnan*, etiologies have two levels of meaning: (a) as a folkloric answer to a natural curiosity, e.g., how did such and such a place, person, or thing get its name, and (b) as a way of legitimating or sacralizing a place by linking it with the person of the Buddha.

12. Interpretation of this sentence is problematic. It is customary to erect tall banners or flags (*tung*) at a wide variety of northern Thai Buddhist merit-making occasions. The custom is also practiced among the Shan and the Lao. Generally it is explained that the length of the flag provides the opportunity for those being punished in the Buddhist hells to grab the tail of the banner and escape from their karmic punishment; that is, the power of the merit generated by the ritual produces a beneficent effect for the dead as well as the living. If the sentence was meant to convey an etiological significance, then it would have attributed the origin of the ritual banner to the Lawa. The *pha sabai* is a folded white cloth worn across the right shoulder, often as a sign of renunciant practice as in *chi phakhao*, or white-robed ascetic. Since conversion is one of the themes in many *tamnan* texts, this sentence could mean that those who followed a non-Buddhist ascetical (Brahmanical) practice became followers of the Buddha.

13. Jotikarama is the Pali name for one of Chiang Mai's major royally sponsored monasteries, Wat Chedi Luang, an important Buddhist site in the history of Chiang Mai from the fifteenth century onwards.

14. One *sok* equals one cubit or approximately 17–21 inches in length. I shall render *sok* by cubit.

15. This passage appears to confirm recent cosmogonic interpretations of the meaning of the stupa or *chedi* built around an axial pillar or Inthakhin.

It is of interest to note that the Inthakhin or Chiang Mai city pillar is currently enshrined at Wat Chedi Luang.

16. Here, and in other northern Thai legendary chronicles, the Lawa are referred to as Tamila.

17. A possible reference to the making of large numbers of votive tablets embossed with an image of the Buddha often encased in a *chedi* or a brick and stucco Buddha image.

18. The text offers the standard apologia for the making of Buddha images, namely, that they function as reminders of the Buddha's presence in his absence. See Richard Gombrich, "Kosala-Bimba-Vannana," *Buddhist Studies in Honor of Walpola Rahula* (London: Gordon Fraser, 1980); Lewis Lancaster, "An Early Mahayana Sermon About the Body of the Buddha and the Making of Images," *Artibus Asiae* 36 (1974), 288–291; Malcolm David Eckel, *To See the Buddha: A Philospher's Quest for the Meaning of Emptiness* (Harper: San Francisco, 1992).

19. Yom cannot be identified with a known location.

20. The Jetavana Monastery donated by the lay disciple, Anathapindaka, appears in many canonical and non-canonical Theravada texts.

21. According to Pali commentarial history, the Buddha died when he was approximately seventy years old, not eighty.

22. Fang, north of Chiang Mai, was an early Tai center in northern Thailand.

23. The Buddha's prediction reflects the historical tensions that existed between the Tai capital of Lan Chang (in modern Laos) and the Tai of the Lan Na region which included various Tai city-states such as Fang, Phayao, Nan, Lampang, as well as Chiang Mai, the dominant Tai state in the north.

24. Today the image is located at Wat Phra Non in the district of Saraphi, Chiang Mai province, just south of the city.

25. Insufficient information is given in the text to identify this site. It is reasonable to assume that it was near a small stream which at one time flowed into the Ping River and then dried up. The attention in the text given to rice paddy irrigation suggests that sufficient water for flooding paddy fields was a concern for farmers. Placing a Buddha image in the middle of a rice paddy is similar to putting a spirit house in a field for the purpose of protecting the field and ensuring a good rice harvest.

26. Doi Tap Tao is north of Doi Chiang Dao, the most important sacred mountain site between Chiang Mai and Fang.

27. Literally, "one who hears the dharma." In this text lay followers of the Buddha are referred to as those who take the precepts, listen to

the Buddha's teaching, attend to the monks, and support the *sangha* with material goods.

28. Phayao is located northeast of Chiang Mai and was one of the early Tai settlements in northern Thailand. Mountains are traditional sites for sages, ascetics, shamans, and various types of magical and religious practitioners.

29. The point of this odd episode seems to be that the Buddha, knowing the time of his death was near at hand, could not have taken medicine that would have brought him back to health. Thus, while the details surrounding the Buddha's death in this *tamnan* depart significantly from the traditional Pali account of the Buddha's death, as in that story, the Buddha is not medicated and dies of food poisoning.

30. This episode appears to be loosely based on the *Devadhamma Jataka* (also found in the commentary on the *Dhammapada*) in which a demon who guards a pool was given permission by Vessavana to devour those who go to the pool who do not know what it means to be truly god-like (*deva-dhamma*). The details of our story differ significantly from the Jataka. We have rendered *deva-dhamma* as "godly meaning" of the material elements of earth and water. This vignette provides a window into the nature of the Buddhist transformation of folk tradition: (a) the Yakkha, a pre-Buddhist mythological figure, requests a Buddhistic interpretation of the two material pre-Buddhist cosmological elements, and (b) a relatively sophisticated Buddhistic epistemology is embedded in the simple, folkloric nature of this episode.

31. A self-enlightened Buddha who does not teach the dharma.

32. Kawila ruled Chiang Mai from 1781 to 1813.

33. Explicit references to the Buddha's vomit and excrement may offend the modern, idealized view of the Buddha as a heroic renouncer. Popular Buddha biographies such as this northern Thai *tamnan* are at a far remove from such antiseptic, rationalized constructions. Making the Buddha's excrement or mucus into relics dramatizes the sacred power represented by all parts of the Buddha's body. Underlying this view is the generalized belief that material objects represent or contain the essence of a being whether human or supernatural, or, in other terms possess manna-like power. Consequently, certain objects may be polluting such as a woman's undergarments, while other objects such as a cloth touched by a holy monk, may be regarded as empowering or protective.

34. Doi Ang Salung is located in the Chiang Dao district of Chiang Mai province. In this text the title, Hariphunchai, seems to be a generic term for

the entire Chiang Mai region of northern Thailand. In some instances it is synonymous with the title, Yonok.

35. Although *tamnan* is usually translated as "chronicle" or "legendary history," it may also be used in an even broader, generic sense of "teaching" or "text." In Thailand the collection of *paritta* ritual texts are known as *tamnan*. In the *Tamnan Ang Salung*, the preacher is the Buddha and the audience is the king who will rule in Hariphunchai from Chiang Dao during the third millennium after the Buddha's death.

36. The Buddha is addressing the righteous ruler who rules from Chiang Dao in northern Thailand associated with the names Yonok and Hariphunchai.

37. *Miang* is made from fermented tea leaves and frequently chewed after meals as a digestive aid.

38. Hongsawadi was the center of Mon power in central Burma before and after the rise of the Burmese in Pagan.

39. Ava was a powerful Burmese state in the Mandalay region in the sixteenth century.

40. Ayodhaya could refer to several different locations but as the text makes clear below, in this case the name is associated with the Laotian kingdom of Lan Chang (Luang Prabang) which flourished between the fourteenth and sixteenth centuries.

41. It is difficult to explain the identification of the righteous ruler (*dharmaraja*) with people who sell costly *miang*, salt, betel leaves, and rice unless one speculates that the writer of the text was making a connection between wealthy merchants and the righteous ruler because merchants sponsored the writing of the text or, in more general terms, were the major supporters of the *sangha*. The meaning may be symbolic but, unfortunately, the text provides no definitive interpretative clues.

42. In the text, the terms Yonok and Hariphunchai both refer to northern Thailand. The geographic locations of the five *dharmaraja* follow an approximate chronological sequence: Asoka's India; the Mon of central Burma; the early Tai kingdom in northern Thailand; the Lao kingdom of Lan Chang with its capital at Luang Prabang; and the Burmese capital at Ava.

43. Dvaravati is the name given to the Mon who dominated central Siam and Burma before the advent of the Tai and Burmese, and whose influence extended into northern Thailand and Laos.

44. The text here is imprecise and confusing. The writer has introduced the concept of the *dharmikaraja*, and associated it with two important

kings—Asoka and Aniruddha—as well as four major kingdoms or city-states of the tenth to the sixteenth centuries: Hongsawadi (Pegu), Hariphunchai (Lamphun), Lan Chang (Luang Prabang) and Ava (Mandalay). He is halfway through the text and needs to move on to Chiang Dao. The fact that the writer earlier identified the Yakkha as the righteous ruler of Hariphunchai and now identifies him with Chiang Dao may be mitigated by the term Yonok. It is associated more generally with the greater Chiang Mai valley which includes both Hariphunchai (modern Lamphun) and Chiang Dao.

45. Place names of locations in India are freely ascribed to locations in Buddhist Southeast Asia. In this case Kosambi may refer to Keng Tung in the Shan States of Burma.

46. Since the text gives only the northern Thai year name (*sak/pi*) with no Chulasakarat date it is not possible to provide a year designation.

47. A peak of 1,930 meters exists at the village of Ban Pha Daeng near Fang but this site cannot be identified with Din Daeng Mountain in the text.

48. The name of Prince Siddhattha's horse when he made his great renunciation.

49. Hariphunchai was a Mon-Lawa center conquered by King Mangrai in 1281. Eventually, Mangrai established his kingdom at the base of Doi Suthep Mountain and called his city Chiang Mai. Chiang Mai was to become the dominant Tai city-state in northern Thailand. Hariphunchai, however, continued to be an important ritual/religious center. Neighboring chieftains swore allegiance to the rulers of Chiang Mai at the Wat Phra That Hariphunchai reliquary in Lamphun. The inclusion of Chiang Dao within the kingdom of Hariphunchai may be intended to refer to the ritual/religious unity represented by the term.

50. A replica of a Kanlapaphruek tree is often erected at large temple fairs. It resembles a giving or wishing tree. For a donation one takes a number from the tree and receives a prize in the manner of a lottery.

51. Indian Rose tree (*mesua ferrea).

52. This may refer to the Flower Garden Monastery (Wat Puppharama in Pali or Wat Suan Dok in Thai), a major royal monastery in Chiang Mai.

53. The Pali term, *adhitthana*, conveys "resolve" or "determination" in the sense of directing or concentrating power. *Adhitthana* was appropriated into Thai with a very similar meaning.

54. Probably a reference to Wat U Mong (the Cave Monastery), also known by the Pali name, Wat Veluvanarama.

55. Burmese obviously were present in the Chiang Mai area when the *tamnan* was written. Reference to Burmese ascetics suggests that the text

was subsequent to Burmese suzerainty of the area after 1558. Regarding the etymology of Chiang Mai, the Thai term, *chi*, is the Thai equivalent of the Pali *anagami or anagamin*, "not returning" or "one who has not returned" and, hence, an ascetic. In an unusual etymological move the author derives, *chiang*, (i.e., town, city) from *chi*. A more standard derivation of *chiang* is from *wiang* which refers to a circular protective wall that defines and protects the town.

56. The term used in the text is "Tamil-lawa."

57. Small flags made from cloth or paper are used in a variety of auspicious ritual occasions while long banners are a distinctive aspect of northern Thai festivals.

58. The symbol of revolving wheels is associated with the concept of the king as world ruler (*chakkaphat*).

59. The text explicitly refers to many Lawa and to only one Burmese. The reason for this numerical distinction is unclear other than a common sense notion that the Lawa were the majority group in the area and the Burmese a smaller minority. Other references to Burmese in the text mention specific numbers, e.g., seven Burmese monks, rather than to the Burmese as an unspecified group.

60. Probably refers to Wiang Kum Kam, King Mangrai's capital before building Chiang Mai.

61. A possible reference to Doi Kham on the outskirts of Chiang Mai.

62. The text contains a long section describing an apocalyptic age when the usual patterns of nature and social conventions are seriously disrupted and in may cases essentially reversed. As in the canonical *Agganna Suttanta* ("Book of Genesis"), a righteous ruler serves as an agent of order in chaotic times. As befitting chaos, perhaps, the compiler of the *tamnan* gives no particular order to the list of problems rampant in this dark age. War, natural disasters, the moral disintegration of all classes of society including the monastic order occur at random.

63. The scene described in the *tamnan* could be interpreted as an imaginative mythologizing of the mysterious formations within the Chiang Dao cave.

64. Sanguan Likhsit, *Tamnan Tham Luang Chiang Dao* (Chiang Mai: Suan Prung 2515 B.E. (1972 C.E.), pp. 10–19. Translated by Donald K. Swearer.

65. Possibly a thinly veiled historical reference to Burmese incursion into northern Thailand.

66. Phramaha Sathit Tikkhayanna tells a different version of the story of Chao Luang Kham Daeng and the golden deer (*Phrawat lae Nam Thiao*

Chom Tham Luang Chiang Dao, (Tharathong: Chiang Mai, n.d.), pp. 54–59, and in the English language version, *History and Guidebook to Chiang Dao Caves* (Santipap: Chiang Mai, n.d.), pp. 42–45. In his account, based on interviews with elders in the area, there are multiple transformations between the female human and animal appearances.

67. This version of the story provides no background for this cryptic reference to Chamathewi, the ruler of Hariphunchai. In *Phrawat lae Nam Thieo Chom Tham Luang Chiang Dao*, Chamathewi is Chao Luang Kham Daeng's wife and dwells at Doi Nang, to the north of Chiang Dao. Although married, they do not live together as husband and wife because both observe the eight precepts. It would appear that the legends connecting the Mon queen Chamathewi, Wasuthep, and the Lawa chieftain Wilangkha are associated with mountains in the Doi Suthep range while Chao Luang Kham Daeng and the ascetic, Brahma, are linked primarily to Doi Aung Salung Chiang Dao. In memory, if not in actual written text, Chao Luang Kham Daeng and Chiang Dao occasionally appear in legends associated with the Doi Suthep range. Chao Luang Kham Daeng is also one of the guardian spirits called upon to join in and protect the buffalo sacrifice ritual performed annually during the month of May/June at the base of Doi Kham to propitiate the Lawa guardian spirits, Pu Sae/Ya Sae. For a translation and analysis of the *Chamathewiwong*, see Donald K. Swearer and Sommai Premchit, *The Legend of Queen Cama* (Albany, N.Y.: State University of New York Press, 1998).

68. In *Phrawat lae Nam Thiao Chom Tham Luang Chiang Dao*, the shrine in front of the cave was not built by Chao Luang Kham Daeng's father but by the villagers. In this version the prince simply disappears into the cave. He is not killed and does not become a Yakkha. The shrine is connected with his comings and goings in and out of the cave.

69. Today the gathering of spirit mediums at Doi Chiang Dao which usually takes place around the time of Thai New Year does not include an offering of live animals, whereas the offering to Pu Sae and Ya Sae, the guardians of Doi Suthep, includes the sacrifice of a buffalo.

Chapter IV Doi Suthep: Wasuthep Mountain and the Legend of Doi Kham

1. Phrakhru Paladphin Kittiwano, *Wat Phra That Doi Kham: Tamnan lae Prawat* [The Legend and the History of the Monastery of the Buddha's Relic on Doi Kham] (Chiang Mai: Phloika Press, 2536 B.C./1993 C.E.). The author

based his account of legends associated with Doi Kham on a book published by Sutthawan Suvannaphat.

2. Translated by Donald K. Swearer and Sommai Premchit. Headings have been inserted for purposes of clarity.

3. Refers to the four paths (stream-enterer, once-returner, never-returner, *arahant*), their fruition, and nirvana.

4. The Buddha Dipankara is the first of twenty-four Buddhas preceding the Buddha Gotama enumerated in the *Buddhavamsa* (The Lineage of the Buddhas).

5. The ten perfections (*parami*) are: generosity, good conduct, renunciation, wisdom, effort, forbearance, truthfulness, resolution, loving-kindness, and equanimity. The superior and supreme perfections are higher degrees or expressions of the same virtues.

6. The Buddhist cosmology includes human, divine, demonic, and animal realms. The divine and demonic realms are populated by various beings over whom the Buddha exercises suzerainty.

7. In this version the male Lawa guardian figure, Pu Sae, is omitted.

8. The six higher knowledges (*abhiñña*) are: magical powers, divine ear, telepathy, retrocognition, divine eye, knowledge of the elimination of all mental intoxicants.

9. One *sok* is one cubit, the length from the elbow to the end of the length of the fingers or approximately 17–21 inches.

10. Relics and consecrated Buddha images are believed to be the real presence of the Buddha, not merely a symbol. Consequently, the relic is "invited" to enter a shrine as though it were the Buddha.

11. We translate *matthalunga-dhatu* as skull bone although conventionally *matthalunga* refers to the brain.

12. This description implies that Sumana established a new sect through ordinations and the reconsecration of ordination halls.

13. Two important northern Thai chronicles, the *Mulasasana Wat Suan Dok*, and the *Jinakalamali* Pali chronicle, do not mention the story of the division of the relic. One might infer that the story was an invention to legitimate the importance of Wat Phra That Doi Suthep.

14. At this point the text continues with a chronicle of kings with special reference to their sponsorship of Wat Phra That Doi Suthep.

15. In the text the reference to a reign is always followed by "and then died." We omit this repetitive phrase. For the Lan Na rulers of the Mangrai dynasty and their reign dates according to the *Chiang Mai Chronicle* and the *Jinakalamali* see Hans Penth, *A Brief History of Lan Na* (Chiang Mai:

Silkworm Books, 1994), 40–42. There are significant disparities between the *Tamnan Phra That Suthep* and the genealogies in these two records.

16. We have abbreviated this section of the text. The dimensions and other numbers in this section differ significantly between the palm-leaf manuscript translated by Swearer and Sommai and the published text (*Tamnan Phra Paramathatsuthep* (2490 B.E./1947 C.E.). We have made some alterations to the translation of the palm-leaf-manuscript version based on the published text.

17. The Mahapadana Sutta (*Digha Nikaya*) enumerates seven Buddhas of the present age including Gotama, and in the *Buddhavamsa* Gotama is preceded by twenty-four Buddhas. The future Buddha, Metteya figures prominently in apocryphal texts, and acts of merit-making often include the wish to be reborn during the time of Si Ariya Metteya. The sacrality of Doi Suthep is enhanced by associating it with the lineage of Buddhas past, present, and future.

16. In popular Theravada belief five thousand years after the death of the Buddha his relics will reappear. Associating this tradition with Doi Suthep further reenforces the sacrality of the mountain.

17. Temporary ordination, often for three months or one rains retreat, is the customary norm in Thai Buddhist practice. In recent years life-time ordination has become an aspect of reformist Buddhist sentiment as, for example, in the case of the Dhammakaya movement.

20. A word-play reference to Chamathe-wi.

21. In other accounts Chamathewi allows Wilangkha three tries to hurl his spear from Doi Suthep to Hariphunchai.

22. In other accounts Wilangkha's strength is depleted when he wears a hat presented to him by Chamathewi made from one of her undergarments.